ST VINCENT DE PAUL, LIVERPOOL

A BRIEF HISTORY AND GUIDE TO THE CHURCH OF ST VINCENT DE PAUL, LIVERPOOL

MICHAEL O'NEILL

GRACEWING

First published in 2013 by
Gracewing
2 Southern Avenue
Leominster
Herefordshire HR6 0QF
United Kingdom
www.gracewing.co.uk

ISBN 978 085244 795 6

Typeset by Gracewing

Cover design by Bernardita Peña Hurtado

CONTENTS

---

6 · St Vincent de Paul, Liverpool

ACKNOWLEDGEMENTS

N 1952, THE Parish of St Vincent de Paul, Liverpool, marked the centenary of its foundation by the publication of a short, illustrated History produced by Mr L. W. Kennan and Mr J. T. McDonnell. This new History seeks to update the story they told and to deepen it by utilising a wide range of primary source material.

It would not have been possible to produce this work without the help of many people, to all of whom I am deeply grateful. Special thanks are due to Dr Rory O'Donnell for his advice and suggestions; to Monsignor Peter Cookson, Monsignor Peter Ryan and Canon Gerard Hetherington, for help with the earlier drafts; to Dr Gerard Hyland particularly for help with original press accounts; to Dr Meg Whittle, Liverpool Archdiocesan Archivist and the staff of Liverpool and Lancashire Record Offices for their patience and support; to Fr Michael Fisher, Archivist of John Hardman and Co; to Mr David Nathan of Northern Industrial Photography who provided all the photographs; and to Sybil Williams and Rachelle Williams-Monaco who word processed the entire manuscript. My wife, Sue, has been unfailing in her support. Any errors are my responsibility alone.

Michael O'Neill
September 2012

INTRODUCTION

MY INVOLVEMENT WITH St Vincent's church goes back over many years to when I was Member of Parliament for the Liverpool constituency of Edge Hill. Towards the end of the 1980's, the structural condition of this great building, which had always served a very deprived area of inner-city Liverpool, began to give rise to serious concerns. As approaches were made to English Heritage for initial funding to help to stabilise the building, a group of Patrons of St Vincent's was set up, including the late Duke of Norfolk, Lord St John of Fawsley and myself with the aim of securing the building in the service of future generations. Over twenty years later, it is good to see how much has been done with walls, roof and interior restored and work now awaited on the belfry and the tracery of the west window. E. W. Pugin and Bernard O'Reilly gave us at St Vincent's a building which has long proved its worth as a catalyst for the local community; it is good to see that all the work so far completed is helping it to continue with its transformational role in the twenty first century. There is no-one better than Michael O'Neill to tell this story and how appropriate that it should be told during the 200th anniversary year of the birth of E. W. Pugin.

David Alton (Professor Lord Alton of Liverpool)
House of Lords, London

1

THE ESTABLISHMENT AND GROWTH OF THE PARISH

HE PARISH OF St Vincent de Paul was created to serve the religious educational and social needs of the rapidly growing Catholic population of south Liverpool. This was to be the twelfth mission in the city, where the oldest mission dates back to 1707. The population of Liverpool in general grew very rapidly in the 1840s, primarily because of immigration from Ireland and particularly during the years of the Irish Famine, 1846–49. Between May 1846 and December 1847, 296,231 Irish people were calculated to have settled in Liverpool.

The rapid growth of the Catholic population outstripped the ability of the existing south Liverpool churches of St Peter (1788) and St Patrick (1821) to serve their needs; in January 1843, Father Parker, Parish Priest of St Patrick's, opened a chapel-of-ease for his church. He rented some former stables at the corner of Blundell Street, which had been converted into a 'penny theatre'. Mass was said there for the first time on 5 February 1843, and accommodation was provided in the same building for 200 children to be taught by one Christian Brother. A priest from Derry, Fr McCormack, volunteered to serve the Chapel-of-

Ease; Mass was at 10 o'clock on Sundays and up to 400 worshippers could be accommodated.

Gradually, the chapel caused the surrounding district to assume a new identity.

By 1848, the Catholic population of the future St Vincent's district had grown to 7,500 and worship was transferred on 23 January from the temporary chapel in Blundell Street to a converted shed ninety feet by thirty, located in Norfolk Street. This second building was also a Chapel-of-Ease to St Patrick's.

On 4 August 1852, however, this chapel was formally separated from St Patrick's and became the parish church of the new mission of St Vincent de Paul. Fr Edward Walmsley was appointed as the first missionary rector. His appointment is noted in the Liverpool Ordo (Annual Yearbook and Diocesan Guide) of 1853.

DIOCESE OF LIVERPOOL

Comprehending the Hundreds of west Derby, Leyland, Amounderness, Lonsdale south of the Sands, and Lonsdale north of the Sands, and the Isle of Man.

Population of Lancashire, 2,063,913. Of the Isle of Man, 52,116. The population of the above-named Hundreds not known.

Right Rev. GEORGE BROWN, Bishop; consecrated August 24, 1840; translated from Tloa, September 29 1850. Residence, Sandfield Park, west Derby.

†‡ LIVERPOOL, Warren Street, Copperas Hill, Cathedral Church of St Nicholas (1812) Very Rev James Provost, Crooke, James Nugent, –Carr, and John wallwork, On Sundays, Mass at 7½, 8½, 9½ and 11; V. and Catechism at 3; Rosary and

Benediction at 7½. On Thursdays, Benediction at 7½ p.m. On W.Ds, Mass at 7½ and 9.

†‡ _____ , Park Place, St Patrick's (1821–24) Edward Kenrick, Pierse Power, Bernard O'Reilly and Roger Arrowsmith.

Mass on Sundays at 7½, 9 and 11; Benediction at 6. On Holy Days, Mass at 5, 8 and 10; V. at 7. On Wednesday evenings Benediction at 7.

Measures have been taken to erect a new chapel in or near Norfolk Street, as the population of that part has become too numerous to be efficiently attended from St Patrick's. The Rev Edward Walmsley and Rev John Aylward are nominated to this new mission. They both reside at No.23, Upper Pitt Street.

The Ordo gives no details of services at this new chapel but we know (Appendix 1) that by 1855 the Norfolk Street Chapel had four Sunday Masses: 7.30; 8.45; 10.00 and 11.00. It seems to have become even busier than its mother church of St Patrick's.

Fr Walmsley, of the Norfolk Street Chapel, died of fever on 23 November 1852 and was replaced by a curate of St Patrick's, a man of outstanding vision, Fr Bernard O'Reilly, who became the second missionary priest. In October 1855, he provided the bishop with a formal Visitation Report on his parish and its temporary church in Norfolk Street; his fascinating report on the dreadful condition of his chapel is given as Appendix 1.

His detailed report helps to explain Fr O'Reilly's ambition to build a permanent, worthy church for his people. He had already held a public meeting at the Clayton Hall on 20 May 1854, to launch his new project, and with the support of (coadjutor) Bishop Goss, a team of thirty men began a weekly, door-to-door collection to raise the necessary funds. An extract from the Pastoral Letter of Bishop George Brown of 15 February 1854 and Fr O'Reilly's letter of 29 October 1854 gave impetus to this appeal and may be read in Appendix 2.

A prominent site was purchased at the junction of St James Street and St Vincent Street (now Hardy Street) for £6,000 with the help of the wealthy Liverpool Catholic businessman, Edward Challoner, and on 6 April 1856 Bishop Goss laid the foundation stone. Each ship's carpenter in the parish laid a day's wages on the stone, and £250 was collected on that first day. The young Edward Welby Pugin, 1834–75, was commissioned to design the new church; the builders were Messrs Thomas Haigh and Sale of Liverpool; Painswick stone was used in the construction of the interior; and the estimated cost was £6,700. Building progress is recorded in the Diocesan Ordo of 1857. The details may be found in Appendix 3.

The new church was opened on 26 August 1857 by five bishops—the Bishops of Dromore (Ireland), Almira (Syria), Shrewsbury and Salford, led by Bishop Alexander Goss of Liverpool, in whose heart St Vincent's always seems to have had a special place. Details of fundraising appeals for the building of the church may be found in Appendix 4, press accounts of the progress of the construction of the church in Appendix 5, and details of E. W. Pugin's designs for the church in Appendix 7. Bishop Goss died on 3 October 1872; his successor was Father O'Reilly who, protesting his unworthiness, was consecrated on 19 March 1873, as third Bishop of Liverpool by Archbishop Manning of Westminster assisted by nine other bishops including Bishop Robert Cornthwaite and Bishop James Chadwick. Bishop O'Reilly was reluctant to leave St Vincent's, and, for a time, used the large adjoining Priest's House (also by E. W. Pugin) at 13, Hardy Street, as his residence, as may be seen from the extracts from the Catholic Directory of 1874 which may be found in Appendix 6. At the same time was consecrated Roger Bede Vaughan OSB, brother of the Cardinal, who went on to be second Archbishop of Sydney.

As Bishop of Liverpool from 1873 to 1894, Bernard O'Reilly approached the development of his diocese with the same vigour as he showed in building St Vincent's. During his episcopate, forty two new parishes and many new churches were opened, and the number of secular priests increased from 133 to 255. He took particular pride in the opening of the diocesan seminary, St Joseph's College, Upholland, on 22 September 1883; and in 1894 he was buried there. Nevertheless, St Vincent's held a very special place in his affections, and continues to hold a special place in the history of the Archdiocese of Liverpool, because of the vigour with which he applied himself first to the work of the mission and later to that of the diocese, particularly in the service of the poor.

Bishop O'Reilly's successors as Parish Priests or missionary rectors (to 1905) of St Vincent's were:

- Father Patrick Flynn 1873–1888
- Father John Oldham 1889–1908
- Father Richard Ryan 1908–1926
- Father William Hodson 1927–1948
- Father Hugh O'Donoghue 1948–1960
- Father Thomas Rattigan 1961–1970
- Father Bernard Wyche 1970–1974
- Father Gerard McClean SCJ 1974–1977
- Father Gerard Giblin SCJ 1977–1982

- Father Thomas Stanley SCJ 1983–1986
- Father Michael Hughes SCJ 1986–1997
- Father Patrick Foley SPS 1997–2001
- Father Kenneth Hyde 2001–2008
- Father John Southworth 2008–

2

WHAT TO LOOK FOR AT
ST VINCENT DE PAUL'S

The Presbytery

T IS A Grade II Listed Building. The presbytery, by E. W. Pugin, is to the north side of the church. It dates from 1856 and is constructed of brick and stone, with a slated roof, in the Gothic style. There are two storeys over basements with gabled attics and tall chimneys. The exterior consists of a broad stone staircase with stone-mullioned windows of three or four lights, having cusped heads and arched hood-moulds, and one oriel window. All the windows have trefoil heads. Other significant features are the niche in the north-west angle of the presbytery wall and the metal railings. The interior of the presbytery has a splendid dining/interview room with dining table, and chairs bearing the motif SVP, together with an open hall having a timber open-well stair and a concealed viewing squint to check on unexpected visitors. It is an important example of E. W. Pugin's domestic architecture.

The Church Exterior

In thirteenth-century Gothic Geometric style, the Church is also a listed building at Grade II*; it is built of stone, executed in rock-faced courses. Upholland sandstone has been used for the walls and the dressings are from the Stourton Hill Quarry.

The plan of the church consists of a six-bay nave with large clerestory windows; a two-bay chancel; and north and south lean-to aisles. The south aisle has gabled windows. The high pitched nave roof is interrupted by cross-gables housing large clerestory windows, repeated on the lower level chancel roof, both slated. They give the building its prominence in the streetscape. The main west front of the church has a large eight-light window with Geometrical tracery. Below, the main west portal consists of paired arched doors under a pointed relieving arch and a traceried roundel in the tympanum just below the arch. The sculpted head to the south of the doorway is that of Bishop O'Reilly; that to the north is of the twentieth century Archbishop Whiteside. The foundation stone upon which the workmen placed their day's wages may be seen in the external wall below the main east window. Perhaps the most striking external feature is the open traceried iron lantern bellcote with its short spire, which springs out of the gable of the apex on the west front. The top of the spire is 120 feet above ground level. The bell was supplied by Murphy's of Dublin. It weighs ten hundredweight, cost £85–0–0 and was inaugurated on 12 July 1857. A close inspection of the bell in situ from the viewing platform of a cherry picker, early in 2012, revealed what may be a previously forgotten misunderstanding. While the inscription on the bell, showing the dedication of the church, should read 'Sancte Vincente de Paul Ora Pro Nobis' it actually says 'Sancte Vincenti et Paule Ora Pro Nobis' as may be seen from the photograph of the bell. How the misunderstanding arose is unknown. E. W. Pugin (unlike his father) delighted in such 'show' west fronts as often no other facade was visible.

The Church Interior

The interior of the church is described in an article in *The Builder*, 1 August 1857. It measures 150 ft. from the west doors to the east wall, sixty two feet from the north wall to the confessional doors and ninety feet from the north wall to the south wall at the rear of the confessional corridor. The height of the nave is fifty six feet and that of the chancel forty nine feet.

The six bays of the nave are separated from the side aisles by octagonal pillars of Painswick stone having foliated capitals. In addition to the realistic carvings of leaves and fruit, one capital on the south side also incorporates a shield containing the Irish harp; another, the Red Hand of Ulster.

The pillars support lanceolate arches having hood-moulds with four (now gilded) angel stops on each side. Each angel holds a shield, some depicting tools, two with open books and one with a set of initials. The carving is probably by R. L. Boulton.

There are 216 panels in the polygonal panelled roof, each framed in wood. This wagon roof is supported by tall wall piers resting on carved corbels, of which thirteen are carved to represent various men's faces. The fourteenth, inside the organ case, is uncarved. A large number of carved heads and other foliated decorations may be seen at the bases of pilasters and on arches above windows and fonts; on each side of the sanctuary, a bishop's head looks down. Above the head on the south side is the coat of arms of Bishop Alexander Goss (1856–72); above the head on the north side is that of Bishop George Brown (1840–56).

The sixth bay at the west end of the nave is occupied by a choir gallery below the west window which fills the west end from the gallery to the church ceiling with elaborate tracery. A continuous wooden music desk fronts the gallery across the entire width of the nave. In the south west corner is located the Gray and Davison pipe organ, at least as old as the church, but of early nineteenth-century style. The three towers and two flats of pipework are formally cased; and of its two manuals and pedals, the Swell is now an unusual survival, terminating at Tenor C. There are eighteen speaking stops and the tracker action was fully restored in 1978. It has been awarded the Historic Organ Certificate of the British Institute of Organ Studies.

The interior of the church is characterised by its clerestory windows, which flood the building with light. Ten four-light leaded, traceried windows light the nave; two pairs of two-light leaded, traceried windows illuminate the choir gallery. The bottom panel of each of the latter is filled with stone, perhaps to accommodate the organ which, however, only occupies the south west corner of the gallery. The eight-light west Window is leaded; the east Window is twenty two feet wide and has nine lights below elaborate tracery which includes a rose window, at its apex. The entire east window is filled with what is thought to be Belgian stained glass which was installed in 1925 by Fr Ryan to replace the previous clear glass. From north to south, the nine lights depict St Patrick, the Archangel Michael, St Vincent de Paul, two Angels, the Virgin Mary, two Angels, St Andrew, the Archangel Gabriel and St George. Above, the eight angels each hold individual invocations from the Litany of Loreto (prayers using titles for the Virgin Mary such as 'Tower of David', 'Gate of Heaven', 'Morning Star'); within the rose, sixteen angels radiate in glory from the central panel, depicting the Lamb of God.

The sanctuary is two bays deep; two gabled clerestory windows, each of four lights, are situated above its north and south sides. These are paralleled by the five clerestory windows above each side of the nave. Four further gabled windows are located in the south wall, above the confessionals, each having spherical triangular tracery; and two three-light traceried windows in the north wall overlook the garden in Hardy Street. The upper part of the west wall of the north aisle contains a large, four-light traceried and leaded window; a similar window is located at the west end of the south aisle, adjacent to a three-light window in the south west corner. Thus, Pugin filled his church with light, most dramatically in the sanctuary.

The sanctuary is separated from the nave by its soaring chancel arch of Painswick stone, fronted on each side by a canopied pedestal containing statues of the Virgin Mary and St Joseph. It is separated from the side chapels by a double arch on each side, each having quatrefoil piers, and filled with oak screens erected by Fr Hodson as a memorial to the 1939–1945 War. The altar rails with their brassed gates separate the sanctuary and the side chapels from the main body of the church; they are constructed of marble and alabaster and were installed in 1916 to commemorate Fr Ryan's

Silver Jubilee (1890–1915). The High Altar is of white marble; its carved front and sides were completed in 1927 in memory of Fr Ryan, but in the same style as the 1850's work, perhaps following details of the temporary altar which must have been here.

Integral with this altar, the reredos is one of the most outstanding features of the church and one of the most important survivals of E. W. Pugin's altar ensembles. The lower half of the reredos consists of a triple arcade on either side of the altar; the central arch on each side allows access to a passage behind the altar, which connects the presbytery (on the north) to the Sacristy (on the south side). The upper half of the reredos designed by E. W. Pugin in 1867 with carving by William Farmer, consists of ten pinnacled, crotcheted and gabled niches in alabaster, separated from each other by a choir of angels and each containing a carved stone statue of a saint. The statues include St Dominic, St Mary Magdalene, St Thomas of Canterbury, St Joseph and St Vincent de Paul (north Side) and the Virgin Mary, St Patrick, a bishop in nineteenth century dress, St John the Evangelist and St Kentigern (south Side). At the centre of the reredos is a tall canopy, perhaps completed later, supported on marble pillarettes, terminating in a spire and framing the Benediction throne. Below the throne, the Tabernacle is of marble with a brass door. The reredos is thought to have been completed by 1867. A special feature of the high altar is its brasswork, especially the six large twisted candlesticks and the cross on the throne.

Originally, the sanctuary floor, which has been replaced, was identical to the side chapel floors, made of oak and Spanish chestnut, arranged in geometrical parquet designs; it was intended for the Earl of Shrewsbury at Alton Towers, but with the Protestant succession to that title in 1856, it came back on the market. Much of the seating, taken from the presbytery dining room, is the work of E. W. Pugin.

The Lady Chapel is situated at the east end of the north aisle. There is a four-light stained glass window by Hardman of Birmingham behind the altar. Depicting the Virgin Mary, the window was installed by the Sisters of Mercy who served the parish for many years from their convent in Great George Square. The Caen stone altar shows the Annunciation, and above the central statue of Our Lady of Lourdes, a steeple-like canopy rests on marble pillarettes. Below is a jewelled, brassed tabernacle. The altar was opened by Bishop Brindle, an Old Vincentian (and the son of one of Fr O'Reilly's collectors), in 1899 as a memorial to Bishop O'Reilly, and can be given to Pugin and Pugin. On the north wall of the chapel are gabled canopies containing three carved stone statues, resting on stone wall brackets. Between the statues is some blind arcading; a window above them provides a 'squint' view of the altars from the presbytery.

St Joseph's Chapel is situated at the east end of the south aisle. Measuring twelve feet by twenty four feet, it is almost identical to the Lady Chapel. There is a leaded, four light window behind the altar which is built of Caen stone and was erected in January 1918 as a memorial to the dead of World War I. In a manner similar to that of the Lady Altar, the painted statue of St Joseph stands below a central steeple-like canopy with an adoring angel to each side and a brass tabernacle below. On the south wall of the chapel are three further canopied stone statues of saints. The altar is also the work of Pugin and Pugin.

The south aisle contains eight arched doorways giving access to the four original confessionals. Each pair of doors is set below a section of blank arcading surmounted by a gabled, three-light leaded window. The larger door at the top of the aisle, adjacent to the statue of St Patrick, leads to the sacristies which contain stained glass, carved wooden vesting presses and a marble lavabo. Above is the former Guild Room, sometimes used as a day chapel; below, a small vault. In the bay at the west end of the south aisle is the shrine to St Vincent de Paul, designed by Pugin and Pugin, erected in January 1930 and presented by the Cunningham family. William Cunningham was Headmaster of the Boys' School 1922–1948. The south west corner of the church is illuminated by the two traceried, leaded windows adjoining at right angles, one of three lights, the other of four. Nearby is a plaster statue of the Scourged Jesus of the late nineteenth century. On the south wall there is also a wall-hung marble-framed picture of St Gerard Majella together with a statue of St Jude and a picture of Our Lady of Perpetual Succour. The fourteen Stations of the Cross are shared between the south and north walls. They are oil paintings in rectangular frames of a typical late Victorian design. The ninth is a replacement following fire damage in the 1960s; the arched door below housed a Lourdes Grotto before the fire but has now reverted to its original purpose of providing a side exit.

The pulpit is adjacent to the south aisle, situated next to the first pillar at the south east corner. It appears to be constructed in Caen stone and the work of E. W. Pugin. It is approached from the south aisle by a circular stone staircase having a banister with trefoil-headed arched openings. In front, two carved stone angels flank the reading desk, honouring the Word of God.

The north aisle contains a number of shrines. At the top, the shrine of the Little Flower was erected by Fr Hodson and the Women's Confraternity. A keen woodworker, Fr Hodson may have helped in its construction; the relic underneath should be particularly noted. Along the north wall are also located statues of the Sacred Heart and St Anthony, and a wall-mounted representation of Veronica's Veil. At the west end of the north aisle is the circular staircase giving access to the gallery; railed into the north west corner of the aisle is the baptistery, overlooked by a large oil painting of Christ's baptism in the River Jordan. Pugin's original design for the church included a hexagonal baptistery to be built at the junction of St James' Street and Hardy Street; it can be seen in his drawing of the exterior, a copy of which is included as Figure 16 in this History. At the time, a house stood on the proposed site; it was eventually demolished, but the baptistery was never built. Outside, the arch may be seen in the south wall which would have linked the baptistery to the main church. Inside, the font, the work of Pugin and Pugin, waits as close as possible to where it was intended to be. The octagonal font is of stone with carved relief panels on its sides and a wooden cover having metal handles and strapwork. It rests on a central pedestal surrounded by four short green marble pillars with carvings of leaves above. The floor tiles depict fish and flowers and the baptistry is separated from the rest of the church by metal railings. It was presented to the church by John Alfred and Anne Kelly of Nile Street in February, 1900. Their son Joseph (1882—1953) grew up in Nile Street, was ordained in 1907 and died as Parish Priest of Sts Peter and Paul, Great Crosby. The west wall has a traceried, leaded, four-light window, matching that at the end of the south aisle and directly illuminating the font. Adjacent to the baptistery is a large Mission Cross, erected in 1861 and an arched doorway in the north wall gives access to the garden.

The floor tiles and benches throughout the church were installed in 1928; the small gilt crosses and brass candlesticks on the walls commemorate the consecration of the church in 1960.

In designing the church of St Vincent de Paul, Pugin adapted the Revival Gothic style, subsequently developed at the church of Our Lady of Reconciliation, Liverpool (1859–60) which established an influential formula for Catholic church planning in the second half of the nineteenth century. By planning very wide naves and equally wide but short sanctuaries, he placed the congregation in dramatic visual relationship with the Mass and especially the very popular Benediction service. His 'town churches'—here and especially at Our Lady's, Eldon Street—achieved as *The Tablet* put it 'a complete revolution in church architecture', reconciling mid nineteenth century Catholics to the continued use of the Gothic style. The particular importance of St Vincent de Paul in these terms is that it constitutes an ensemble that has not been re-ordered.

3

Some Parish Personalities and Activities

I. Personalities

(i) Bishop Bernard O'Reilly was born at Ballybeg, Co. Meath on 10 January 1824, the son of Patrick O'Reilly and Mary Blundell. His Irish background may be commemorated in the symbolic harp and red hand in the foliated capitals in the south arcade.

After ordination by Bishop Riddell in 1847, he served as curate at St Patrick's—where he contacted typhus in the epidemic of 1847, but was nursed to recovery by Canon Maddocks at Old Swan—and he took responsibility for St Vincent's in 1852. His younger brother, Gerald, was ordained in 1856 and after three years as curate at St Vincent's was Rector of St Mary, Wigan until 1873 and of St Oswald, Ashton-in-Makerfield until his death in 1896

(ii) Bishop John Patrick Barrett was born in St Vincent's Parish in 1878. After education at St Edward's College and Oscott, he was ordained in 1906. After further study and work in Paris, he taught at Up Holland and Oscott until becoming Auxiliary Bishop of Birmingham in 1927. From 1929 until his death in 1946 he was Bishop of Plymouth and is buried at Buckfast Abbey.

(iii) Bishop Robert Brindle DSO was born in Christian Street, Liverpool, in 1837 and grew up in Blundell Street. Trained at Lisbon, he was ordained in 1862 and first served at Westminster Cathedral before transfer to the Diocese of Plymouth. At the age of thirty seven, he became an army chaplain and served in the unsuccessful military campaign to rescue General Gordon at Khartoum in 1884. After a distinguished military career, in which he became the first chaplain to win the DSO, he became Auxiliary Bishop of Westminster in 1899 and Bishop of Nottingham in 1901–15. After his death in 1916, he was buried at Nottingham Cathedral with full military honours.

(iv) Fr Richard Ryan was born in Guilcough, County Kilkenny, in 1866, the son of Patrick Ryan and Margaret Hartley. After education at St John's, Waterford and Up Holland, he was ordained by Bishop O'Reilly in 1890. He was curate at St Joseph, Preston, 1890–97, St Bede, Widnes, 1897–1900 and Rector of St Joseph, Peasley Cross, 1900–03 and of St Patrick, Barrow, 1903–08. Thereafter, as Parish Priest of St Vincent's until his death in 1926, he provided strong leadership for his parish, which is commemorated in the interior fittings of the church. He is buried at Ford.

(v)Fr William Hodson was born in Preston in 1876, educated at Ushaw until 1919, and ordained in 1905. After a period as Prefect at Ushaw until 1919, he became curate of Our Lady of Mount Carmel, Liverpool until 1926 when he succeeded Fr Ryan as Parish Priest of St Vincent's where he continued until his death in 1948. He composed the words of the Hymn to St Vincent, still used in the parish and set to music by Fr Charles Rigby.

(vi) Thomas Burke, 1865–1941, a cousin of Bishop Barrett, was born in St Vincent's Parish and baptised by Canon O'Reilly. He took an active role in the political life of Liverpool, eventually becoming an alderman. His 'Catholic History of Liverpool', published in 1910, remains a standard work on the development of nineteenth-century Catholicism.

(vii)John Bridge Aspinall, 1818–86, Barrister and Recorder of Liverpool, was, for many years, deeply involved with St Vincent's Parish. His obituary, in the *Liverpool Review* of 13 February 1886, states that he 'raised himself by his rare abilities to a position of national eminence ... he was a devout religionist and a decided strength to the Roman Catholics...'

(viii) William Radcliffe, VC, MM, 1882–1963, is the only Vincentian known to have been awarded the Victoria Cross, which was won because of his outstanding bravery at Messines on 14 June 1917. On his return to St Vincent's Parish, the schoolchildren presented him with a gold watch on 30 August 1917, and sang a specially composed song. He received his Victoria Cross from King George V in October 1917; subsequently he lived in Brindley Street. He is buried in Allerton Cemetery, Plot RC 19:274.

(ix)Curates who have served in the parish include:

Fr McCormack	1843	Laurence Power	1864
Richard Grayston	1847	William Walsh	1865
William Fayer	1847	John Aylward	1865
John Aylward	1853	Richard Kennedy	1865
Richard Seed	1855	Richard Baynes	1869
Peter Holmes	1857	Joseph Fagan	1870
Gerard O'Reilly	1859	John Kelly (Secretary to	
Michael Donnelly	1860	Bishop O'Reilly) 1874	
Francis Bartley	1863		

Thomas Drum	1874	Charles McCabe	1926
Patrick Duff	1874	Walter Ormsby	1928
Edward Lupton	1877	Hugh Fitzpatrick	1930
John Layne	1880	Hugh Gildea	1940
James Eager	1880	John Clayton	1940
Humphrey Kerrin	1881	Denis Canny	1941
Francis Gillow	1882	Anthony Roney	1944
William Haimes	1883	John Moriarty	1950
James Birchall	1884	Kevin Mulhearn	1956
Edward Lavelle	1888	James McLaughlin	1958
John Swarbrick	1888	James Anderson	1960
John McEneiry	1891	James Beirne	1969
Michael Coffey	1897	James Matthews	1976
James Walsh	1898	Bernard Pidcock	1976
James Mather	1904	Fechin McCormack	1977
William Hickey Junior	1904	Joseph Lee	1978
Henry Conway	1912	James Boyd	1983
Wilfred Alcock	1912	Peter Flanagan	1984
Michael Twomey	1917	John Hindley	1998
James Prescott	1918		
John Dee	1919		
William Sweeney	1923		
George J. Sargent	1926		

(x)Vincentians currently serving as priests:

Canon Gerard Hetherington (ordained 1964) retired Parish Priest of Petersfield.

Fr Joseph Robinson (ordained 1963) now Parish Priest at Burscough Hall, Lathom.

II. Activities

(i)The Schools

Christian Brothers staffed the first school in Blundell Street and continued to work at St Vincent's Schools until 1884. At first, they taught in the Norfolk Street building which also served as a church; later, a former Methodist chapel in Jordan Street was adapted for use as a school, Edward Challoner paying the costs of £4,360. This building came into use on 10 January, 1859, being opened by Bishop Goss. Edward Challoner always tried to give what he could to charity during his lifetime rather than to leave money after his death, and declared a special interest in the children of St Vincent's, whom he entertained one day each year at his home in Old Swan until his death in 1874. This annual event may be the predecessor of the later St Vincent's 'Treat'. Bishop O'Reilly offered Requiem Mass for this great benefactor of St Vincent's who was buried below the Sacred Heart altar of St Oswald's Church.

In 1868, new schools were built in Norfolk Street to replace those in Jordan Street, and named the 'Challoner Schools'; in 1898, they were extended by Dean Oldham. Following the departure of the Christian Brothers in 1884, the Boys' School came under the control of lay teachers, and the Girls' and Infants' continued to be served by the Sisters of Mercy, who in 1885 also developed the St Vincent's Select School, firstly at Great George Square and later at their convent at 20, Hardy Street until it was damaged in 1940. In 1903, St Vincent's Schools came under the authority of Liverpool Education Committee.

After the Second World War, it was decided to construct new schools, to be shared with St Peter's Parish, on a site in Greetham Street. When this work was completed, the Challoner Schools in Norfolk Street were used for parish social activities, but were eventually demolished. At the same time, new and larger secondary schools for those aged over eleven years were provided—outside the parish—so that in 2009 the Greetham Street/Pitt Street site is the base for a Primary School serving the needs of 179 children led by Mr P. Stewart.

(ii) The Treat

The Treat, as such, no longer exists. Its origins lie in the annual entertainment provided by Edward Challoner for the schoolchildren at his home in Old Swan. After his death, the parish continued to organise an annual day out for the children. First known as 'Dockers' Day', it later became known as 'The Treat'—the day when schools and shops closed, houses were decorated, and the whole parish marched behind its band to board the train to Southport for a day's entertainment. This colourful annual event had ceased by 1970.

APPENDIX 1

Archive Material

Fr. O'Reilly's Account of his Temporary Church, October 1855

The present church is situated in Norfolk Street, Liverpool. There is no property whatsoever connected with it. The sacristy is a corner boarded off at the Gospel side of the altar.

Originally, the present shed (the church) was held by lease for an unexpired time from Edward Challoner, Esq. I believe that the time is now expired but I have not been able to learn and we now hold it at his good will. It is charged with a yearly rent of £15–0–0.

The church is an oblong room, ninety feet by thirty feet. It will accommodate about 500. There are sittings for 300. The sittings are the same as one used on Weekdays as seats and desks for the schoolchildren. There is standing room for about 200. There is no gallery.

I do not know when or how the shed was built. It is built partly of old bricks; the rest is fenced in with old boards and in parts with corroded sheet iron. There is no tower, no steeple or belfry, no bell, no cross. The sanctuary is formed by boarding off a portion at one end. This is divided into three portions; those at the sides being used as sacristies and confessionals, the centre portion, ten feet by ten feet as a sanctuary. The ceiling is perfectly open, it is not plastered.

It is covered partly with wood and slates and in parts with mortar, pitch and tar. The church shows damp in every part. Hardly any part of the roof will keep out the wet. In wet weather, the walls and partitions are generally streaming with water to such an extent that at times we have to make holes in the floor to drain away the water. The roof is such that it could not be permanently repaired, and the walls and supports could not bear a new one. There are eight windows (skylights) in the church. They admit sufficient light. The church is ventilated by four ventilators in the roof, which are generally kept open in all weathers, and by four apertures, two in each gable end, which are also in general kept open except in bad weather. There are two holy water stoups of stone. The church is lighted with gas. In the church there is a stove, which, however, is not in any way serviceable to warm the church. It is of use to the children during school time. There is a gas stove in the sacristy which in damp and cold weather is lighted during the hours of Mass in the morning, as also during the time when the confessional is attended.

The inside of the church is partly brick, partly wood, partly sheet iron. The walls and roof are whitewashed. It is, however, impossible to keep them clean as every shower disfigures them. The sanctuary, or that portion of it which is enclosed by the doors which shut up the altar during such times as the shed is used as a school, was by my order and at the expense of about one pound, papered with oak paper.

The church is floored with boards. It is swept every day after school; a portion near the altar is washed every week; the whole three or four times in the year. There are no graves. I do not know if ever any portion of the exterior wood or ironwork was painted. Everything in and about the church is most miserable and in every way out of repair. I do not think that under present circumstances it could be kept in repair.

There is but one altar in the church and this is dedicated to St Vincent de Paul. There are no other chapels and there is no endowment. The altar is of wood and plain. The altar stone was consecrated by the Rt Rev Dr Goss about a year ago. Its dimensions are eighteen inches x eighteen inches. The altar cloths are changed once a fortnight... the silver vessels are cleaned once a week ... the candlesticks (wooden) once a fortnight. The tabernacle is of wood, lined throughout with white silk. The Blessed Sacrament is not kept there except during the times of service, when there is a lamp kept burning. At other times the Blessed Sacrament is kept in a similar tabernacle in the Domestic Oratory in the house. There is no baptismal font in the church.

There are four Masses in the church in the Sundays —7½, 8¾, 10 + 11. On weekdays there are two Masses —7½ + 8¼. Benediction is given on all Sundays and Holy Days, Feast of St Vincent and each day in May. There are the requisites for Benediction but not belonging to the Mission.

There is a small musical instrument (the Harmonium) in the church. There is a small choir. During the Mission for adults in Advent 1855 over a fortnight 1,800 approached the sacraments.

STATUS ANIMARUM

Families	1680
Souls	7701

Yearly Communions

1853	5835
1854	10195
1855	12209
[1856	11144]
[1857	10750]
[1858	15700]

Baptisms

1852	48
1853	214
1854	232
1855	270
[1856	311]
[1857	265]
[1858	511]

The house does not belong to the Mission. I hold it as a yearly tenant, annual rental £35–0–0. The school is taught on the monitorial system, taught by two Christian Brothers. Fr Kenrick of St Patrick's finances it. There are no annual subscriptions. There is a Night School for Girls taught by Voluntary Teachers from 7–9 on weekday evenings. Attendance is very irregular, fifty or sixty to 150 or 180 … The number of boys on the books is 300 …

APPENDIX 2

Fr O'Reilly's Appeal for Funds, 1854

New Church of St Vincent of Paul,

LIVERPOOL

I venture at this time, as an appropriate occasion, to put forth the claims which the great undertaking committed to my charge has upon the sympathy and support of the Catholic Body.

The District comprises the poor and densely-populated streets running between St James's Street and the Docks. My flock numbers 7,600 souls—two streets alone, New Bird Street and Brick Street, contain each 1,200 Catholics.

For several years past we have made use of a miserable shed for the double purpose of Church and School, and have had to offer up the Holy Sacrifice in a building insufficient to keep out the wind and rain.

It so happens that whilst my flock consists of the poorest of the poor, land in the district is most costly, and it has been the work of years to obtain a site. I have, at last, with the blessing of God, been successful in securing one admirably adapted for the purpose, in the very centre of the district, and upon which I hope very shortly will stand the Church of 'ST VINCENT OF PAUL,' another monument of Catholic progress and another evidence of the Catholic principle of caring for the poor.

I have not yet collected sufficient Funds for the Purchase of the Land, but as soon as this has been accomplished, I propose to commence Building the Church at once, relying upon the charitable support of the Public.

The undertaking has the warm sanction and approval of our venerated Bishops, who take an active interest in this effort to plant another Church amongst the poor, and who have been kindly pleased to point to it as a fitting object for the Charity of the Faithful during the Jubilee.

THE FOLLOWING IS AN EXTRACT FROM DR BROWN'S JUBILEE PASTORAL

> You are fully aware of the very great want of a Church in that part of Liverpool near the Docks, known as the Church of St Vincent of Paul. Notwithstanding all the efforts that have been made to procure the Funds necessary for erecting the intended Church, the amount required is far from being procured. On this account we recommend to all the Faithful to appropriate all their alms during the Jubilee, to the erection of the Church above-mentioned, as being the most meritorious good work to which at present they can be given.

Subscriptions will be gratefully received by the Very Rev Dr CROOK, Warren Street, and by any of the other Clergy.

BERNARD O'REILLY
32, GREAT GEORGE STREET
29 October, 1854

APPENDIX 3

Extract from the Diocesan Ordo, 1857

†‡ Liverpool, St Vincent of Paul's. A temporary mission, till a church can be built, has been opened in Norfolk Street. Revs Bernard O'Reilly, Richard Seed and Peter Holmes, who reside at 32, Great George Street.

On Sundays, Mass at 7½, 8¾, 10 and 11, with Sermon; Catechism Instruction at 2½; Dev. Of Confrat. Of Holy Family (for boys) at 3¼; Baptisms at 3. Rosary, Sermon and Benediction at 6½. On Holy Days, Mass at 5, 7½, 8½ and 9½; Rosary and Benediction at 7½. On W. Ds, Mass at 7½ and 8¼. On Monday evening, Dev. Of Confrat. Of Holy Family (for girls) at 7. On Friday evening, Stations of the Way of the Cross and Benediction at 7½.

'For the last fifteen years, this poor congregation has met for prayer—first, in a miserable garret over a rag store, later, in an almost open shed, previously used as a hut for the storing of timber. During this length of time, week after week have they contributed their pence—many a time in so doing stinting themselves in their scanty meals to raise in time an edifice worthy of their holy religion. The fruit of these years of labour and sacrifice has been expended on the purchase of a site for a church, to be dedicated to God in the name of the "Father of the Poor", St Vincent of Paul, the foundations of which were solemnly blessed by the Bishop in April last. They are therefore left without a shilling to pay for the building now fast in progress, with a debt even now pressing hard upon them, and a heavier debt still in prospect, unless the charitably disposed lend them a helping hand. For the love of Jesus and his Immaculate Mother, of Holy St Joseph and Blessed Vincent, give something, even a trifle, to help the poor mission, of which the late Venerable Bishop of Liverpool wrote, that to his knowledge in his diocese, and to his belief in all England, there was not a more urgent call of charity, or one that had more pressing claims upon the benevolence of Catholics. Give then, a trifle to this poor mission, destitute alike of church and schools, and the blessing of God, which the prayers of eight thousand poor Catholics will merit for you, be your reward. It is hoped that the building may be completed and opened for public service in May or June. A table may supply the place of the altar, and the cast-off vestments of other churches may serve for the priests, unless the charity of Catholics provides better for the Divine worship. The smallest donation will be thankfully received by the Bishop, the Right Rev Dr Goss, St Edward's College, the Rev B. O'Reilly, or the other Pastors, 32, Great George Street, Liverpool.

We bear testimony to the correctness of these statements, and recommend to the charity of the Faithful this earnest appeal on behalf of a church, as dear to us as it was to our venerated predecessors, because it is for God's poor, who have little to offer but their prayers towards the completion of this church.'

ALEXANDER, Bishop of Liverpool

APPENDIX 4

Fundraising Activities

The Committee, in again calling the attention of Catholics to the importance of ministering to the urgent spiritual wants of a poor and densely-populated district like that in which it is proposed to erect the New Church, feel that they can scarcely add any thing to the admirable remarks of the Venerated Bishop of Liverpool, in his last Lenten Pastoral on this subject. They will, however, again venture to remind the Catholic public, who have always cordially responded to appeals similar to the present, that a great number of poor Catholics have no means, or, at least, no other than those which will shortly be taken from them, of receiving the consolations of Religion, and hence of the great necessity there is for erecting a Church in the district referred to in the foregoing Resolutions.

The accommodation already provided is totally inadequate to receive the numbers of Catholics who should attend Divine Service, and there is no doubt that unfortunately too many of the poorer classes of Catholics attempt to justify their lukewarmness and neglect of their religious duties, on the plea that there is no room for them in the Churches already erected. To those not acquainted with the circumstances, it may be proper to state, that the district in question is one in which the Epidemic of 1847 raged with the greatest virulence, and where many of those estimable Clergy, who, like their great Master laid down their lives for their flocks, caught the disease which hurried them to the grave. The temporary building in which the large number of poor Catholics who inhabit the district in question meet to assist at the Holy Sacrifice, is about to be taken away from them in consequence of the termination of the lease, and thus they will be deprived of the means of performing their religious duties, unless some steps be at once taken in their regard. The Building itself is of the very poorest description, not protecting the congregation even from the inclemency of the elements. The Committee, therefore, confidently appeal to that generosity and Catholic spirit which, in this diocese, and more particularly in Liverpool, have raised so many Churches and Schools to the honour and glory of Almighty God. They feel that they have only plainly and truthfully to lay before those Catholics, whom God has blessed with wealth and prosperity, the spiritual necessities of their poor brethren in the faith, to induce them readily to come to their assistance, and to perform a duty the most pleasing to Almighty God, and the most honourable to his creatures, viz.:—that of raising a Temple to his glory. Though above £3600 have been already collected or promised, yet the value of the land in the neighbourhood where it is proposed to build the Church is so high, that this amount will not suffice to pay for the land alone.

Contributions will be gratefully received by the Rev BERNARD O'REILLY, 32, Great George Street; the Very Rev Provost CROOK, 16, Warren Street, Liverpool; or by any Member of the Committee.

B. O'REILLY, CHAIRMAN

At a PUBLIC MEETING of the CATHOLICS OF LIVERPOOL, convened by the authority of the Right Reverend DR BROWN, Bishop of Liverpool and held at the CLAYTON HALL, on TUESDAY, 16th MAY. 1854, to take measures for the ERECTION of the NEW CHURCH OF ST VINCENT OF PAUL, in one of the Poorest Districts in Liverpool.

THE RIGHT REVEREND Dr BROWN IN THE CHAIR;

It was Moved by J. B. ASPINALL, Esq., Seconded by The Very Reverend PROVOST CROOK, and *Resolved,*—

That the Erection of a Catholic Church in the District of which New Bird Street is the centre, is the work of the highest order of Catholic Charity, the great number of Catholic Inhabitants, and the general poverty of the District, giving it especial claims upon the benevolence and consideration of the whole community.

Moved by RICHARD SHEIL, Esq., Seconded by the Rev C. H. COLLINS, SJ, and *Resolved,*—

That recognising, as we do, that the Poor are at all times the particular objects to be cared for in God's Church, we determine to Build a Church in this District, and we urge on the whole community the importance of co-operating with their Venerated Bishop in a work so truly Catholic.

Moved by DANIEL POWELL, Esq., Seconded by the Rev JAMES SHERIDAN, O.S.B., and *Resolved,*—

That, to carry out the foregoing Resolutions, a Subscription be now entered into, and that the following
Gentlemen be requested to act as a Committee, to assist
the Rev BERNARD O'REILLY in Collecting Funds and
Building the Church:–

CHAIRMAN—THE REV B. O'REILLY

MR H. SHARPLES,   MR JOHN YATES, JUN,
MR D. POWELL,   MR G. LYNCH,
MR J. B. ASPINALL,   MR T. RYAN

TREASURER—THE VERY REVEREND PROVOST
CROOK
SECRETARY—MR THOMAS DALY

LIST of SUBSCRIPTIONS RECEIVED at the MEETING, the great Majority of the Subscribers having already given largely:

	£ s. d.		£ s. d.
Mr. M. Macklin	100 0 0	Mr John Browne	5 0 0
" H. Sharples	50 0 0	" J. Quinn	5 0 0
" D. Powell	50 0 0	" Haggerty	3 0 0
" R. Sheil	30 0 0	" J. O. Wood	2 2 0
" J. Gibson	20 0 0	" James Reade	2 0 0
" R. Cusker	20 0 0	" B. Mahon	2 0 0
A Gentleman	10 0 0	" S. Burns	2 0 0
Mr. E. Dunne	10 0 0	Rev. E. J. Bradshaw	1 10 0
" R. Dunne	10 0 0	Mr. J. C. Griffin	1 1 0
" T. Darwin	10 0 0	" William Connolly	1 1 0
" J. Yates, Jun	10 0 0	" William Splaine	1 0 0
Messrs. Rockcliff & Sons	10 0 0	Rev. Thomas Kell	1 0 0
Mr. Peter Garvey	10 0 0	Mr Owen McKenna	1 0 0
" Jameson	6 0 0	" James Reade, Jun	1 0 0
" J. Mullins	5 5 0	Very Rev. John Canon Walmsley	1 0 0
" W. Baynes	5 0 0	Mr. P. O'Keefe	1 0 0
" J. B. Aspinall	5 0 0	" Stephen Benville	1 0 0
" T. Moynagh	5 0 0	" O'Donnell	1 0 0
S. H.	5 0 0	" P. Lynch	1 0 0
Mr. J. Lennon	5 0 0	" V. J. Verbraeken	1 0 0
Messrs. G. & J. Lynch	5 0 0	" M. Rice	1 0 0
Mr. T. Carroll	5 0 0	Rev. Jas. Sheridan	1 0 0
" B. Traynor	5 0 0	Mr. Jas. Clarke	1 0 0
" E. Kelly	5 0 0	" Rourke	1 0 0
" J. Doyle	5 0 0	" Giacomo Lertroi	1 0 0
" G. Stewart	5 0 0	" Charles Crangle	1 10 0
" T. Daly	5 0 0	" J. Newton	0 5 0
" D. Bannon	5 0 0		
" M. Carney	5 0 0	£476 14 0	
" R. H. Sheil	5 0 0		
" W. Bunbury	5 0 0	Sundry Collections at Meeting	8 0 11½
" W. Reynolds	5 0 0		
		£484 14 11½	

Previous to the Meeting the amount in hand was............£2799 13 5
Sum promised before Meeting.....................................£352 0 0
TOTAL...£3151 13 5

To this amount, of course, will have to be added, the amount promised and received at the Meeting.

APPENDIX 5

Press Accounts of the Construction of St Vincent's Church

From *The Tablet*, 12 April 1856, p. 229

DIOCESE OF LIVERPOOL
(*From our own Correspondent*)
Liverpool, April 9th, 1856.

We have little more than a solitary fact of any interest this week in Liverpool; but it is one of those facts that illustrate a year and benefit generations unborn. A new church has been founded under the patronage of Saint Vincent of Paul. The beginning of its story dates back half a dozen years. The Rev. Bernard O'Reilly was at that time attached to the important Church of St Patrick, where he was known as a hard worker, always at his post, sound in judgement, prompt in determining, and persevering in execution. During the dreadful fever scourge, which carried off most of our Priests, Father O'Reilly was twice prostrated by typhus; but, thanks to a good constitution, 'the brave heart within', and his having still a great work to accomplish, he was almost miraculously restored to his old sphere, and was soon in the thickest of struggle. He did not fail to observe that there was a large district towards the south end of the town sadly in want of religious appliances, as there was neither church nor Pastor further that way than Saint Patrick's. The Unitarians built their new church in a more *respectable* part of the town than that in which they wont to congregate, thus vacating their former chapel in Paradise-street. A faint effort was made towards buying this place for a Catholic church, the very attribute that rendered it unpleasing in the eyes of the Unitarians being its chiefest recommendation to the Catholics. However, it came to nothing; and the chapel was bought up at last for a music saloon and beerhouse. *Qualis erat, quantum mutatus ab illo !* The famous council of the wise men of Gotham consulted half a day, and at last concluded that something must be done. Father O'Reilly did the same, but he went further, and did it. He began by detaching himself from St Patrick's, and plunged straightway into the midst of his elected garden. To this end he hired a capacious shed in Norfolk-street, and fitted it up as a chapel, on Mahomet's principle, 'If the mountain won't come to Mahomet, Mahomet must go to the mountain.' If the people won't come from their homes to the chapel, the chapel must go amongst their homes to them.

Father O'Reilly's chapel was a dreadful object to all lovers of eau-de-cologne, and the lowest Churchmen in England couldn't object to incense as being a useless mummery there of a hot summer Sunday. Nothing about it was endurable, except the altar service; that was never rich, but it was always beautiful and clean, if poor. All this time the poor Paddies were gathering those magic pennies of theirs that have raised more churches than the coffers of her Majesty's Treasury and the cellars of the Bank of England. While cotton has been rising and falling, and railway shares have been now above par and anon below it, the Norfolk-street money market of a Sunday evening has been steady, and no want of confidence was ever felt that the end would be attained at last. No obstacles can conquer the *justum ac tenacem*, and at last Father O'Reilly paid 6,000*l.* for the ground. This made it his own, or rather the church's, for ever; it was bought freehold and unencumbered from any sort of rent or lordship whatever. This was the first act; the second came off yesterday in laying of the foundation stone, and we trust we shall soon have to put on record 'the last scene of all,' when the labours and anxieties of the Priest shall be closed by the solemn dedication of his glorious church.

The site of the new building is St James's street, which is the main thoroughfare of the south end of Liverpool. It seems that the town council felt some alarm lest a conspicuous building, occupying so prominent a spot, might not be worthy of its position, and expressed a wish to have the plans submitted to their inspection. As an act of courtesy Father O'Reilly consented to this, and sent the plans in. The beauty of the design soon dissipated all imaginary fears, and drew from a member an avowal that the Catholics in building their churches did not generally do things by halves.

In the evening the Irish Club held their annual dinner party at the Adelphi hotel. St Patrick's Day is the usual term for this meeting; but as March 17th happened this year to be a Monday in Holy Week, the festivity was very properly adjourned to the day on which the Church celebrates the great Saint's office.

The cloth having been withdrawn, and the usual formal toasts proposed and rapturously received.,

The CHAIRMAN again rose and gave, 'The Bishop of the Diocese and the English Hierarchy.' (Loud cheers.) He wished to say a few words of the Right Rev. Prelate on his right. (Loud applause.) He felt it an honour to preside at a dinner where his Lordship sat for the first time since his inauguration as the Bishop of Liverpool. (Cheers.) Though all of them, when they reflected on the character of their late Bishop, his services to the Church, and knew the zeal and energy he brought to bear on everything Catholic, they must feel proud that they had one so well able to follow him in his good and wise example. (Applause.) He did not think it out of place to refer to the energy and zeal with which the present Bishop had taken up this matter, which the late eminent Dr Brown so ardently desired. Ever since he had been made Bishop his zeal and energy had been directed to the promotion of Catholic objects in this town. (Applause.) He (the chairman) being officially connected with the new Church of St Vincent de Paul, had found his Lordship's wish was always to be amongst the poor of his flock. (Applause.) He had been in that district on all occasions, encouraging the collectors by his counsel and his blessing. As that was the first official dinner which Lordship had attended, he felt they would wish most cordially that Heaven should shower upon him its choicest benediction, and that he might be long spared to carry out those objects for the benefit of the church which were in progress, and that he might long have health and strength to spread religion by his example and his precept. He concluded by proposing the toast of—

'The Bishop of the Diocese and the English Hierarchy.' (Cheers.)

His LORDSHIP then rose and said he begged to thank them for the very kind manner in which they had received his health. He was not easily appalled, but yet he confessed he felt somewhat bewildered at the manner in which they had received the mention of his name. He had thought they would be afraid of hearing him, for this was the fourth time he had spoken today. In each of the previous speeches he had had occasion to praise, and to praise with great pleasure, the energy of the Catholics of Liverpool, and he had appealed to the great works which they had already achieved in the number of their churches, of their schools, and in the increase of their Clergy. They could not traverse the streets by day or by night without feeling convinced that still much more was required at their hands. (Hear, hear.) By day they found the streets crowded by ragged urchins, who were sent out to get a livelihood as they best could. (Hear, hear.) But a great many of them were not in the habit of attending any school. They had, in the first place, to provide school accommodation for them, although, at the same time, they had school accommodation to a greater extent than was made available; in other words, their schools were not made available as far as they might, and, therefore, their first effort would be to make use of the schools as far as they could be used, and then to raise others, for he believed that one-half of their children were unacquainted with what was termed secular knowledge. If they traversed their streets by night they found them in a disgraceful state, crowded with unfortunate persons who had lost their virtue, and then, being deserted by their friends, they had been cast abroad upon the streets to earn their livelihood by the wages of sin. (Hear, hear.) Yet they must feel there were many of them who felt their degradation, and were anxious to retrieve themselves, and would accept to go into an asylum were there one provided for them. (Hear, hear.) Now, whilst they discountenanced to the fullest extent the vicious lives they were living, yet at the same time they could not but feel commiseration for their lives, for they knew their Blessed Lord himself treated with compassion people of that habit of life. (Hear, hear.) They had great need of a reformatory school, for, unfortunately, the reformation was busy amongst them, and many of their children would be kidnapped in the streets, and sent to a place where they indeed reformed from vice, but where probably they would lose their religion. (Applause.) That day they laid the foundation of a new church—a church for the working people—(loud applause)—a church which he trusted would be raised by the working people alone, for up to this time they had received little assistance from those to whom they had perhaps a right to look for more. He therefore hoped they would go on and persevere, so that they would have the satisfaction of knowing that by their own unaided energy they had themselves raised a church for their accommodation. He trusted also that the day was not very far distant when they might again be called together to lay the foundation stone of another church—cathedral for this diocese. (Loud applause.) They must not be satisfied with building churches where they were imperatively demanded, but at the same time build a church which would be worthy of God who would be adored in it, and which would not be merely large enough for those who would habitually frequent it, but would be spacious enough to hold the whole of the Catholics of the town, whenever they might be called together for a great occasion. (Cheers.)

The Tablet, 28 February 1857, p. 131

FROM OUR LIVERPOOL
CORRESPONDENT

A distressing accident occurred a few days ago since to a labourer engaged in the erection of the new Church of St Vincent of Paul; he fell from the top of the roof of the nave, and unsuccessfully attempting to save himself by catching at the ridge, was thrown to the ground; he was found to have sustained a fracture of the thigh of such a nature as, upon his removal to the hospital, to render amputation necessary. The poor fellow still remains in a most precarious state.

For the information of such of your readers as feel interested in the progress and erection of new churches, which happily are gradually taking the place of the 'conventicle' 'concert-room' buildings, in which we have been accustomed to worship for so many years, I beg to furnish you with some account of the state of the building above referred to. The Church of St Vincent of Paul is now rapidly advancing towards completion; it is nearly covered in, and already forms a most pleasing and interesting object in the midst of the shops and warehouses which surround it, calculated to lead the mind of the beholder from the worldliness which the neighbourhood presents to the contemplation of that great Creator, whose glory will dwell within that earthly tabernacle. The style of the church is that of the ornamented Gothic; the architect is Edwin Pugin, Esq. It is situate in the St James's-street, and consists of nave and aisles, with spacious sanctuary and side chapels, dedicated respectively to the Most Blessed Sacrament, and St Joseph, and to Our Blessed Lady, with confessionals and sacristies, over which is a room for the use of confraternities, &c. The church is designed to accommodate about 1,200 persons. At the north-east corner is the spacious presbytery. A porch and baptistery are included in the design, and will be erected hereafter at the north-west corner. The stonework of the windows is complete, the proportions of which have been much admired, especially the rose in the east window. The clerestory windows have been designed with great boldness and much beauty, and will make up for the deficiency of light, occasioned by the proximity of other buildings precluding any windows in the basement. The builders have contracted to finish the church in early June, and it is the anxious desire of the Clergy to open it in the course of the ensuing summer.

This account of the progress of the church may be interesting to many who are already acquainted with the circumstances of this poor mission; but there are others who may be totally ignorant of the wants of this district, to whom a further explanation of the causes which have led to the partial erection of this beautiful church may not be altogether uninteresting.

The parish, the spiritual wants of which this church is destined to supply, has been found, by a recent census, to contain 8,000 souls. The present chapel, which on Sundays is used for Divine Worship, and on week days for a school, will accommodate 300 persons; thus, with five Masses on a Sunday, only 1,500 out of 8,000 souls can hear Mass, and it is feared that the residue live without complying with that sacred obligation, for the late venerated Bishop Brown, in his Lenten Pastoral for 1854, after bringing the spiritual destitution of this parish prominently before the Faithful, and earnestly exhorting all in the diocese 'to unite their contributions, and concentrate all their energies on this object alone, until it is completed,' adds emphatically:—'Let it not be supposed that they may find the consolations of religion in other churches—there is no room for them—the churches are full to overflowing.' The site upon which the new church is now building being considered most eligible, situate as it is in the very centre of the parish, was purchased, the sum of 7,000*l.* being paid for it, which totally absorbed the weekly collections which for some time had been made amongst the poor congregation, consisting 'of small shopkeepers, of labourers depending for their subsistence upon casual labour at the docks, of fish and fruit sellers, of venders of chips and sand.' Very little has since been collected to enable the Pastors to pay off any considerable portion of the debt, for which they will be responsible when the church shall be placed in their hands by the contractors; but of the sum contributed, 5,000*l.* has been collected 'in the pence of the poor.' This church, which in the double sense may be called the 'church of the poor,' dedicated as it will be to that Saint of comparatively modern times, who is appropriately called 'the father of the poor,' and erected mainly by 'the united mites of the poor,' appeals loudly for assistance to that favoured portion of the Faithful whose spiritual wants are more amply provided for, and who, blessed with the riches of this world, we are looking around for objects desirous of their charity at this holy season. In the Rev. Bernard O'Reilly, of 34, Great George's Street, Liverpool, the Pastor of this poor struggling flock, who have done their utmost to help themselves, the Faithful will find a grateful recipient of their alms; and they will, at the same time, be helping the work of the Lord in one of the most distressed portions of His vineyard.

St VINCENT OF PAUL, LIVERPOOL.—

The Tablet, 18 July 1857, p. 453

On Sunday last Dr Goss, the Lord Bishop of Liverpool, solemnly consecrated the new bell here, after which his Lordship addressed the congregation for more than an hour, during which time nothing could exceed the attention and interest evinced by all present. The church is now all but completed, and forms the most complete and picturesque building in the town, and here is met (with success) one of the principal objections to churches in the pointed style, viz., open roofs; in this case a counter ceiling extends over the entire church, which will, in a great measure, prevent the continual shafts which invariably arise where this precaution is not taken. The house is already occupied, and the church is expected to be opened about the middle of August.

DIOCESE OF LIVERPOOL

The Tablet, 19 August 1857, p. 548

SOLEMN DEDICATION
AND OPENING OF THE
CHURCH OF St VINCENT
OF PAUL, LIVERPOOL.

(*From our Preston Correspondent*)
Liverpool, Wednesday.

I write from Liverpool, whither
I have come to the solemn
dedication and opening of the
new Church of St Vincent of
Paul. It is, as you observed in
the *Tablet* of Saturday last, 'a
great day for Liverpool'—Liverpool, with its thousands and
tens of thousands of Catholics,
to whose eternal weal the erection and opening of this church
are of vastly more importance
than the numerous marts of
commerce, the halls of mer-
chant princes, the docks, the
harbours, the fleets, and golden
argosies which enterprising
and wealth-abounding Liverpool possesses.

The mission of St Vincent
of Paul, for the service of
which this splendid new church
has been raised, and towards
whose erection the poor con-

gregation have week after week
contributed their pence, 'many
a time in so doing,' as has been
stated to us, 'stinting themselves in their scanty meals,'
was established as a separate
mission distinct from St
Patrick's, August 4th, 1852, the
Rev. Edward Walmsley, since
deceased, being appointed to
the charge of it. It had been
served as a station many years
previously by the Priests
attached to Saint Patrick's. On
the 5th of February, 1843,
Mass was celebrated in an
upper room in Blundell-Street,
and on the 7th of February a
boys' school, taught by a Christian Brother, was opened in the
same room. This arrangement
was continued, with the excep-
tion of three months during the
fever of 1847, till January,
1848.

On the 23rd January, 1848,
Mass was celebrated in a large
shed in Norfolk-Street, the
school also being removed
thither. On the 28th of October,
1849, and subsequently, two
Masses were celebrated on all

Sundays. Early in 1852 a second Christian Brother was appointed to the care of the school. The mission embraces nearly the whole of the municipal division of the town of Liverpool known as Great George's Ward, and a portion of that known as Rodney-street Ward. The zealous Priests serving this mission are the Revds. Bernard O'Reilly, Richard Seed, Peter Holmes, and Gerald O'Reilly, each of whom has laboured untiringly, in season and out of season, to complete the undertaking which they have had on hand— viz., 'A church to be dedicated to God in the name of the "Father of the Poor", St Vincent of Paul,' the foundations of which were blessed by the Bishop of the diocese in April, 1856.

Who was St Vincent of Paul, under whose invocation this church has been commenced and dedicated? A great and illustrious Saint, endowed, to use the language of Holy Church, with Apostolic courage to preach the Gospel to the poor, and to promote the beauty of the Ecclesiastical order. Born of poor and humble parents, towards the close of the six-teenth century, the shepherd's boy, who laboured in the fields and tended his father's sheep and swine amid the Pyrenees, who was taken captive and sold as a slave at Tunis, became, and was recognised, as the Apostle of charity, establishing found-ling hospitals, hospitals for the aged poor, and a hospital for the galley slaves at Marseilles. It was St Vincent of Paul who founded the Congregation of Priests, of the Mission (or Lazarists), not confining their Missionary labours to the limits of France, but extending them to Poland, Italy, Barbary, the island of Madagascar, the islands of the Hebrides, to Scot-land, and even to Ireland, where Cromwell's army was then depopulating the country, and committing the most appalling deeds of rapine and bloodshed. To St Vincent of Paul we owe the institution of parochial fra-ternities for the relief of the poor, of the confraternity of ladies for the service of the Hotel Dieu, of Sisters of Char-ity, of retreats, and spiritual conferences, &c. St Vincent of Paul died in 1660, was beatified by Benedict XIII. in the year 1729, and in 1737 was canon-ised by Clement XII. 'St

Vincent of Paul,' says a recent writer of his life, 'still lives in his works; his spirit guides them now. The energy of that dauntless old man cannot die; the love which burned so fervently in his heart is too divine ever to grow old.' We rejoice that the example of his virtues has begun to exert an influence even in England, and that churches, in veneration of his pious merits, are being erected in our great and populous towns, in places where sin, and misery, and human wretchedness most abound, and which our Saint laboured so assiduously to abate and assuage. It is not long since a spacious church was erected in his honour in Sheffield, and now in Liverpool we behold a noble and magnificent church built and placed under St Vincent's invocation. This church, whether we regard the elegance of its design (it is sufficient to state that it was designed by, and carried out under the direction of, Edward Welby Pugin, Esq., and does special credit to the talents of that celebrated architect), its skilful workmanship, its spacious accommodation, and its various other architectural details, is a temple well befitting the sacred solem-

nity of Divine worship, and reflects especial honour of the generous, persevering, and praiseworthy efforts of the poor, who co-operated so zealously and contributed so liberally towards its erection. May it prove to them the source of innumerable blessings, and may their great and holy patron, St Vincent of Paul, obtain for them health, benediction, and reward.

The church is situated in St James-street, Liverpool, in a densely populous neighbourhood, and amidst a poor flock, composed in great part of the Irish population who throng the vicinity of the docks and shipping.

The buildings of which the church, &c., consist, are in the purest style of geometrical Gothic, their greatest feature consisting in extreme simplicity with regard to detail and almost entire dependence on boldness of outline for beauty and effect.

The church consists of a chancel sixty feet wide by twenty four feet deep, which extends the width of the church, so as to afford accommodation for forty communicants at a time (this is a very necessary arrangement for our large towns); two lateral chapels, which occupy the eastern bays of the aisles by means of six equilateral arches of imposing proportions. At the west end of the nave comes the organ gallery, which is reached by means of a spiral staircase in one of the western buttresses. The church has four entrances-one at the west end into the nave, two in the aisles, and one from the presbytery into the sacristies. At the eastern end are three commodious sacristies, with trap doors, and other conveniences for stowing away the Paschal candlestick and other articles of church use.

On the south side are arranged the confessionals for four Priests, which are approached from the aisle by the people, and from a cloister by the Clergy. These are provided with fireplaces and other conveniences.

Over the high altar is the superb east window of nine lights, with its manipulated and ramified circle of twenty feet in diameter. This is divided from the side chapel windows (which consist of four lights, each with elaborate tracery,) by means of Painswick stone arches, elegantly wrought and moulded, and somewhat in the style of St Mary's, Beverley. On the side walls of the sanctuary are rows of well-proportioned canopies to receive figures of Saints. These are at present uncarved, which detracts greatly from the general effect.

The whole of the roofs are constructed of framed principals, with moulded purlins and wall plates, which form the principal divisions to the ceiling. These are again subdivided by smaller ribs, that have a pleasing and good effect, especially the nave roof, with its fine flowing arches, which have almost the appearance of groining.

The floor of the sanctuary is of various devices, composed of Riga oak and Spanish walnut. This floor was intended for the grand banqueting hall at Alton Towers. The nave is lighted almost exclusively from a clerestory of unprecedented boldness among our modern churches, and the effect of light is acknowledged by all to be far softer and better adapted for our churches than the ordinary mode of lighting from the aisles. In the south aisle a kind of dormer, or clerestory windows, have been introduced.

In the absence of windows the aisle walls have been divided into compartments and arcades, in the centre of which will be placed the Stations of the Cross of a telling size.

The floors under the benches are laid with boards, and the aisles with York flags.

The entire church is benched with convenient seats in polished pitch pine.

On the extremity of the west gable is the bellcot, surmounted with an exquisitely-wrought spiret, covered with beaten lead, and ornamented with a gilded cross, finials, gurgoils, &c.

The whole of the external walls of the church are built of Upholland stone in regular-size courses, with Stourton stone dressings.

The presbytery is situated on the north-east angle, and communicates, as we have before mentioned, with the sacristies of the church. It consists of refectory, waiting-hall, five sitting-rooms, and seven bedrooms. The offices, &c., are below stairs, the whole forming a most complete, convenient,

and thoroughly Ecclesiastical edifice.

The contractors for the work were Messrs. Haigh and Company, Fraser-street, Liverpool, the cost of the whole being 7,000*l*.

The length of the church is 128 feet; height, 64 feet; width of nave, 34 feet; of aisles, 13 feet.

The morning (Wednesday) of the day of the opening of St Vincent of Paul's dawned on Liverpool with cheering brightness. The busy streets soon awoke to life; labour and industry again plied their task-work, and the greed of gain and the acquisition of wealth resumed their hold on men's minds, appearing to make up the sole end and aim of their existence. We passed through the motley throng that filled the streets and squares, and, directing our steps to St James's-street, soon found ourselves at the doors of the beautiful church we have above described. Priests and people—the old and young—were entering, and it was soon filled by a numerous and respectable congregation.

The church, without any pretensions to splendour of adornment, was decked with much taste, and hung round with various religious banners. The ceremony commenced at eleven o'clock by a procession of the Clergy, the Religious Orders, the respective Prelates, and their several attendants, who passed up the church to the chancel, headed by the Cross-bearer, Acolytes, &c. The Office of Tierce was then sung, after which commenced Pontifical High Mass, sung by his Lordship the Bishop of Liverpool, Right Reverend Alexander Goss, D.D.

The following Right Rev. Prelates and Clergy were present:—

His grace the Most Rev. Paul Cullen, Archbishop of Dublin and Primate of Ireland; the Right Rev. Cajetan Carli, Bishop of Almira, V.A. of Thibet and Hindostan; the Right Rev. P. J. Leahy, Coadjutor Bishop of Dromore; the Right Rev. William Turner, Bishop of Salford; the Right Rev. James Brown, Bishop of Shrewsbury; the Right Rev. Alexander Goss, Bishop of Liverpool.

The Chapter of Liverpool, represented by the Very Rev. Canons John H. Fisher, D.D.; Thos. Newsham, Henry Greenhaigh, John Walmsley, Edward Kenrick, James Fisher, John Walker, John wallwork.

The Chapter of Salford, represented by the Very Rev. Canons Edward Carter, James Wilding, and John Kershaw.

The Chapter of Shrewsbury, represented by the Very Rev. Canons Ambrose Lennon, James Pemberton, Randolph Frith, Robert Chapman, and Eugene Egan.

Secular Clergy—The Revds. R. Gillow, New House; George Fisher, Appleton; John Carter, Woolston; Wm. Henderson, Yealand; Wm. Arnold, Huddersfield; Maurice Duggan, Thos. Tobin, Peter Magrath, St Joseph's Liverpool; Thomas Roskell, D.D., the Pro-Cathedral, Copperas-hill, Liverpool; Thos. Kelly, St Alban's, Liverpool; John Flynn, Blackbrook; F. Dujardin, St Anthony's, Liverpool; Bernard O'Reilly, Richard Seed, Peter Holmes, Gerald O'Reilly, St Vincent of Paul's, Liverpool; James Carr, Runcorn; James Carr, Isle of Man; John Doherty, Chorley; Thomas Canon Harrison and Timothy O'Connell, St Marie's, Bradford; Robert Turpin, Scorton; James Fleetwood, Liverpool; Patrick Fairhurst, St Alban's, Liverpool; John Coulston, Singdale House, Birkenhead; Robert Cornthwaite, D.D., Rector of the English College, Rome; Henry Jones, Blackrod; William Molloy, Madeley (Shropshire); Peter Baron, Puddington; Thos. Lynch, St Patrick's, Bradford; Stephen Wells, Saint Patrick's, Bradford; Thomas Spencer, Bootle; George Duckett, Wolverhampton; Edward O'Neille, St Chad's, Manchester; Roger Taylor, St Augustine's, Preston; Thos. Wrennall, St Chad's, Manchester; Wm. Wrennall, Joseph Wrennall, Gabriel Coulston, Jas. Taylor, J. Cook, St Cuthbert's College, Ushaw; Wm. Arthur Wilson, Mossley (Yorkshire); T. Bennet, Old Swan; James Nugent, Catholic Institute, Liverpool; P. Laverty, do.; John Gibbons, Maryvale; James Hearsnipp, Poplar; Michael Meehan, Carrigaholt (Ireland); Geo. Fisher, Appleton; T. Walton, Liverpool; William Walton, Alkingham; John Rogerson, Birkenhead; John Aylward, Fleetwood-on-Wyre; Michael Power, Bollington; Patrick Power, Holyhead; S. Walsh, St Anthony's, Liverpool; Patrick Phelan, St Patrick's, Liverpool; Henry England, Birkenhead; T. Crombleholme, Manchester;—Landy,—O'Donnell, Henry Bennett and Richard Holden, Ushaw, &c., &c.

Benedictine Fathers—The Very Rev. Dr Burchall, President, Woolston; Very Rev. Peter Greenough, Prov., Ince Hall; Revds. Wm. O'Sullivan, St Anne's, Edge-hill, Liverpool; Thomas Almond, St Mary's, Liverpool; James Basil Duck, St Anne's, Edgehill, Liverpool; John P. O'Brien, St Augustine's, Liverpool; Wm. Davy, Seel-street, Liverpool; George Caldwell, Little Crosby; William Corbett, Hindley; Thomas Bonney, Seel-street, Liverpool; Thomas Margeson, Wrightington; E. G. Linass, Leyand; P. Dunne, Rexton; Austin Pozzi, St Augustine's, Liverpool; William Scarisbrick, Douai; and Patrick Leavy, Whitehaven.

Jesuit Fathers-Revds.—Francis Laing, St Helen's; William Corry, St Francis Xavier's, Liverpool; Wm. Cotham, Prescott; and Fr. Moran, St Francis Xavier's, Liverpool.

Redemptorist Fathers—Rev. Fathers Lans and Buggenoms, Bishop Eton.

Capuchin Fathers—Rev. Fathers Emidius, Elzear, Lewis, and Alphonso.

Passionist Fathers—Rev. Fathers Ignatius, Provincial; Bernardine, Alban, Joseph, Celestine and Alphonsus.

Oblates of Mary—Rev. Fathers Jolivet, Noble, Bradshaw, Gubbins, Arneux, and Duterte.

Each of the Religious bodies was attired in the habit of his Order, the Capuchins being readily distinguished by their coarse brown habits, sandalled feet, and flowing beards. Assistant Priest to the Lord Bishop of Liverpool, Very Rev. John Henry Canon Fisher, D.D.; Assistant Deacons at the Pontifical Throne, Very Revds. James Canon Fisher and John Canon wallwork; Deacon of the Mass, Rev. Gerald O'Reilly; Sub-Deacon, Rev. Gabriel Coulston, St Cuthbert's College, Ushaw; First Master of Ceremonies, Rev. Thomas Kelly; Second do., Rev. James Taylor, St Cuthbert's College; Assistant Masters of the Ceremonies, Revds. Richard Seed and Peter Holmes; Crossbearer, Rev. Thomas Roskell, D.D.

Chaplain to the Right. Rev. the Bishop of Almira, Rev. Thomas Lynch; to the Right Rev. Bishop of Salford, Rev. Henry Jones; to the Right Rev. Bishop of Shrewsbury, Very Rev. Canon Chapman; to the Right Rev. Coadjutor Bishop of Dromore, Rev. Wm. Arnold; to his Grace the Archbishop of Dublin, Very Rev. Canon Lee, D.D., Dublin.

Cantors—The Revds. Wm. O'Sullivan and John O'Brien, OSB.

Thurifer—Master Wm. Powell, St Edward's.

Acolytes—Masters James Aspinall and Richard Carr, St Edward's.

Crosier-Bearer—Master Austin Powell, St Edward's.

Mitre-Bearer—Master William Gilbertson, St Edward's.

Bugia-Bearer—Master Joachim Pacheco, St Edward's.

Book-Bearer—Master Manuel Charon, St Edward's.

Train-Bearer—Master George M'Intyre, St Edward's.

We may here state that the number of Priests in attendance was about ninety-three.

After the gospel, an eloquent sermon was preached by the Right Rev. Dr Leahy, Coadjutor

Bishop of Dromore, who selected his text from the twentieth chapter of the 1st Book of Paralipomenon. After the sermon and the collection, the usual indulgence was granted by his Lordship the Bishop of Liverpool. The Holy Sacrifice then proceeded, and the solemn service terminated about two o'clock p.m.

The music was under the direction of Mr Richardson, of the pro-cathedral. The choir was very numerous, with full orchestral accompaniments. As the procession entered the church, the choir sang 'Attollite Portas' (Richardson). The Mass was Haydn's Imperial, or No. 3. At the collection was sung 'Cantate Domino' (Croft), at the Offertory 'Gratias Agimus' (Gulielmi). Handel's Allelujah Chorus concluded the solemn and imposing function.

We regret that, owing to the short time available before post, we have been compelled to abridge the latter portion of our account, not being able so much as to refer to the excellent sermon of the Right Rev. Dr Leahy, or to the luncheon, which was given in the Assembly Rooms, Great George-street, and the speeches which followed it. Nor have we time even to allude to the evening service—Pontifical Vespers and Benediction of the Most Holy Sacrament, and to the beautiful discourse delivered by the Bishop of Shrewsbury. We must, however, *en passant*, tender our grateful acknowledgements to the Revds. B. O'Reilly and the other Clergy of St Vincent of Paul's for the kind assistance and attention they have shown us in the discharge of this our pleasing duty to the Catholic public.

The Tablet, 5 September 1857, p. 565

DIOCESE OF LIVERPOOL
OPENING OF St VINCENT'S
CHURCH

[The subjoined report, taken from the *Daily Post*, will supplement the account given last week by our own correspondent]:—

Immediately at the conclusion of the ceremonial at the church, the Bishops, Clergy, and a large number of the congregation, proceeded to the Royal Assembly-room, Great George-street, where a luncheon, at once profuse and tasteful, was spread for their entertainment. The Right Rev. Dr Goss, the Bishop of Liverpool, occupied the chair. On his right sat the Right Rev. Dr Leahy, Coadjutor Bishop of Dromore; the Right Rev. Cajetan Carli, Bishop of Almira, and Vicar-Apostolic of Thibet and Hindostan; and the Very Rev. Canon J. H. Fisher, D.D., St Edward's. On his left sat the Right Rev. the Bishop of Shrewsbury, and the Rev. B.

O'Reilly. Amongst the general company were several ladies.

The repast having been done ample justice to, The Right Rev. Dr Goss rose and said: My Lords, ladies, and gentleman, I feel that I am not in a position suited to me today, and I, therefore, beg to move to the chair the only gentleman present of the committee for the erection of the Church of St Vincent of Paul—Mr Daley. (Hear, hear.) I am sure it requires no recommendation beyond the mention of that fact to entitle him to your acceptance. He was always punctual in his attendance; and, though he might have pleaded the Scriptural excuse for absence, he was never absent.

The motion having been seconded, and carried with acclamation, Mr DALEY, solicitor, took the chair amidst renewed cheers.

The CHAIRMAN said: Ladies and gentlemen, I think it is usual, in assemblies of this kind, to propose the health of the Head of the Church on earth, and I feel that it is unnecessary, in an assembly of Catholics, to preface that toast at any length. (Hear, hear.) All the cant about loyalty, and all that sort of thing, is happily exploded in the present day; and, without further remarks, I give you—

'The Health of His Holiness Pope Pius IX.' (Loud cheers.)

The CHAIRMAN: The next toast in order is, I believe, the health of her Majesty the Queen. (Cheers.) This, too, requires from me no introductory remarks to make Catholics at all times drink the toast with the utmost loyalty and enthusiasm. I give you—

'The Queen.'

The toast was received with great warmth.

Air—'God Save the Queen.'

The CHAIRMAN: I am quite sure you are all anxious to hear the next toast. What we have hitherto done were matters of duty and obligation—pleasing duty, certainly; but the toast I have now to propose to you is one that enlists not only our duty, but our best affections. (Hear, hear.) It is, 'The English Hierarchy and the Bishop of the Diocese.' (Loud cheers.) I

think it would ill become me to make any remarks on such a subject, more especially in the presence of the Right Rev. Prelate and of the large number of his Clergy, who are so well acquainted with the zeal and efficiency with which he discharges his Pastoral duty. (Cheers.) I therefore satisfy myself by giving the toast—

'The English Hierarchy and the Health of His Lordship the Bishop of the Diocese.' (Cheers.)

Air—'The Fine Old English Gentleman.'

The Right Rev. Dr Goss rose, amidst renewed cheers, to respond. He said—My Lords, ladies, and gentlemen, I rise to thank you for the honour you have conferred upon me in drinking my health. I believe, according to the law of the land, I don't exist—(cheers and laughter)—inasmuch as by royal proclamation there is no Bishop of Liverpool. But I am one of those who think that the fact of the Pope having established a bishopric of Liverpool is the surer guarantee of the existence of Liverpool, than the shipping which crowds at its ports. (Hear, hear.) Where is there an instance on record of the establishment of a bishopric by the Pope that the plan has not answered? In many instances where established in small hamlets these have grown into large towns. I might take Durham for instance. (Hear, hear.) No matter for royal proclamations—no matter even for persecution, the see of Liverpool will endure. I have no doubt that the Catholics will resist persecution, and as firmly and as perseveringly as did their ancestors. (Hear, hear.) In the time of Henry VIII. the axe and the stake were tried. The same persecution was continued under the brutal Elizabeth, the wily William, and the sottish Georges. It is only a recent period that we have been comparatively free; but, as I have said, I feel no doubt that, if called upon again to suffer, the Catholics would endure that suffering as perseveringly as before—(hear, hear)—no matter whether the persecution comes from the crown, or from parliament, or from classes of bad people. (Hear, hear.) Now, there is a class of people called select vestrymen, who have taken to persecution in a small way. They are strong, and valorous, and fiery with religious

hate against poor parish children, but cowardly when they come to face men. If called upon to fight the battle against men, and not against children, they might be found imitating that prudent man who got his shield fastened on a part of his body where honourable and courageous men are not accustomed to seek protection. (Loud cheers and laughter.) If we are to have war, we ought to have open war, on persons who could withstand persecution, and not on harmless and innocent children. (Hear.) I hope some effort will be made to rescue the children from this miserable persecution of the select vestrymen, many of whom would be unknown but for their displays of intolerance at that board. But I am wandering from the subject. I wish to say, as I have no existence here by the law of the land—because the law ignores the see of Liverpool—yet I do exist, and trust by your support to continue to exist. I trust I shall be ever with you, and with my brethren of the English Hierarchy, in the foremost of the battle for religious freedom. I have now to thank you for the kindness done to me. I feel that I am not in my element here, as my place is rather in the church; but then, a Priest is always in his place when in the midst of his people, and I feel truly gratified to-day at the attendance of so many of my church brethren from all parts of the country. A Bishop has many trials and difficulties to contend with, but it is always a consolation to reflect that he still numbers in after life amongst his friends the companions of his college course—those who knew him in his early days—who had started with him in the race, and who had watched his career from the beginning; and I, for my part, always feel it to be a greater consolation for me to preserve the friendship of those who were associated with me in early life than to acquire new friendships. (Loud cheers.)

The CHAIRMAN: I shall make no apology; I shall make no preface in proposing the next toast. I content myself with giving —

'The Irish Hierarchy, and the Right Rev. preacher of this morning.' (Loud cheers.)

Air —'St Patrick's Day.'

The Right Rev. the Coadjutor Bishop of DROMORE rose amid renewed cheers. He said—Mr Chairman, my Lords, ladies, and gentlemen, I feel extremely obliged to you for the kind manner in which you received mention of my name in connexion with the toast of the Irish Hierarchy. But, notwithstanding that kindness, I really feel that I owe an apology to you for appearing as a preacher on this great occasion. (No, no.) Oh, I really do; but the circumstances were such as to leave me, I think, no possibility of refusal. There is, perhaps, scarcely a person less inclined than I am to leave the sphere of my immediate duties, which are of such a nature as to claim my whole time and attention. But the Rev. Mr O'Reilly called upon me in Newry, and told me he was searching through Ireland for a whole week for a preacher— that he was disappointed, and that he threw himself on me. (Loud laughter.) Perceiving his candour, and also being informed by a respectable Clergyman who accompanied him that he had effected wonders in this town, and especially for the benefit of my poor countrymen here, I certainly had not the heart, however reluctant I was to accept his offer, I had not the heart to refuse him.

(Cheers.) But whatever reluctance I then felt, I certainly feel now that all has disappeared in the many causes of delight I have here this day. (Hear, hear.) It was to me a delightful thing to see that magnificent church, for which I was totally unprepared, erected by the genius of Mr Pugin and by the labours of the Rev. Mr O'Reilly and the respected committee that assisted him—and I must again repeat what I said before to-day—and by the pence of my poor countrymen. (Loud cheers.) It is also a source of delight to me to have made the acquaintance of his Lordship the Bishop of Liverpool, their Lordships the Bishops of Shrewsbury and Salford, our Right Rev. friend the Bishop of Almira, and the other respected and respectable Clergymen who took part in the interesting ceremony to-day. I had often heard, indeed, of their goodness of heart—and I say it without the least intention of flattering—but I never had the opportunity before to-day of their personal acquaintance. There is another source of delight greater still—that I should have had a share, however insignificant, in the glorious ceremonies of to-day; and I trust I may hereafter have some claim for all the good that may be effected as a consequence. (Hear, hear.) You have coupled my name with that of the Hierarchy of Ireland. This is opening ground on which I feel it very difficult to express myself properly. I am but a very humble member of that Hierarchy, and I take the Hierarchy in its theological sense—Bishops, Priests, and inferior Ministers. I shall confine myself to this. To judge of that Hierarchy, look to their people. (Cheers.) It is true these people have their faults, and it would be hard if, after centuries of persecution, there did not remain some marks of the chain. But with all their faults they stood up for the religion of their ancestors, in defiance of hostility and blandishments; many of them sacrificed their lives, many their properties; they were reduced to be a byword amongst the nations of the earth, but yet they clung to the faith of Christ (Loud cheers.) The fate of Ireland has been indeed disastrous, and it would be unaccountable if it could not come to an end. But the end has not come. Ireland, that adhered so firmly to the Faith, was reduced, I may say, to the lowest depths of degradation and poverty. Famine broke in amongst our people about ten years ago, and I hope none of you have witnessed or shall ever witness such scenes as I then beheld. They now appear to me more like a dreadful nightmare than a reality. In fact, looking back now, I can scarcely believe that such things existed in the nineteenth century in civilised Europe. (Hear, hear.) But I saw human beings in the south of Ireland and in the west of Ireland at the period, and I declare to you they looked more like disinterred bodies covered over with rags picked up from the dunghill, than beings with immortal souls. But God, who thus visited them, had His own wise ends to that calamity. Let us trust that a better hour is dawning upon them now; and whatever their fate, in weal or woe, I trust they will still be able to say, with the Apostle, 'I have fought the good fight; I have preserved the Faith.' (Loud and continued cheering.)

ST VINCENT OF PAUL, LIVERPOOL.—

In the new Church of St Vincent of Paul, Liverpool which we described last week, we omitted to state that the carving of a portion of the stone work is kept in block, so that persons piously and charitably inclined may have an opportunity of carving a cap and head, or whatever they can afford. An example has already been set by his Lordship the Bishop of Liverpool, to whose generosity the church is indebted for the beautifully carved cap on the first pillar in the nave. On the Monday succeeding the opening, Solemn Mass *coram Episcopo* was sung by the Very Rev. John H. Canon Fisher, D.D., and the Bishop of Almira, the Right Rev. Cajetan Carli, D.D., preached. In the evening the sermon was preached by the Right Rev. Dr Goss. At each service the church was attended by a large and respectable congregation.

The Tablet, 8 May 1875, p. 596

LIVERPOOL

St VINCENT DE PAUL'S,
LIVERPOOL. —

On Sunday special services
were held in this church on the
occasion of the unveiling of the
new reredos. The sermon in the
morning was preached by the
Bishop of Liverpool, and the
evening by the Rev. Father
M'Loughlin, C.SS.R, of
Bishop Eton.

Appendix 6

Extract from the Catholic Directory, 1874

DIOCESE OF LIVERPOOL

Comprising the Hundreds of west Derby, Leyland, Amounderness, and Lonsdale in Lancashire, and the Isle of Man.

Patron of the Diocese: Our Blessed Lady, conceived without sin, Dec. 8.

Bishop of Liverpool, Right Rev Bernard O'Reilly, third Bishop: born at Ballybeg, Co. of Meath, January 10 1824; consecrated at Liverpool by the Archbishop of Westminster, March 19 1873. Residence, 13 Hardy Street, Liverpool.

Predecessors:

1. Right Rev George Brown: born at Clifton, near Preston, January 13 1786; consecrated by Bishop Briggs at Liverpool, August 24 1840, Bishop of Tloa and Vicar-Apostolic of the Lancashire District; translated to Liverpool, September 29 1850; died at Liverpool, January 25 1856.

2. Right Rev Alexander Goss: born at Ormskirk, July 5 1814; consecrated by His Eminence Cardinal Wiseman, September 25 1853, Bishop of Gerra and Coadjutor of the Right Rev George Brown, Bishop of Liverpool, whom he succeeded January 25 1856; died October 3 1872.

3. Vicar General

Very Rev John H. Canon Fisher, D.D.

Registrar for deceased Clergy
Rev R. Holden, St Oswald's, Old Swan.

Secretary
Rev John Kelly

†‡ St Vincent of Paul, St James Street W. (April 8, 1856; August 26, 1857). HIS LORDSHIP THE BISHOP; Revs Patrick Flynn, John Kelly, Thomas Drum, Patrick Duff (13 Hardy Street). Sunday Mass, 7, 8, 9, 10. Children, H.M.11; C inst. And B for children 2½; Baptism 3¼, W.Ds 8½, R. Sermon, B 6½. Holy Days, Mass 5, 7, 8, 10; M 10; devs and B 7½. Wkds Mass 7, 8, 9. Thursday evening, B 7½. Friday evening, Sta 7½.

APPENDIX 7

E. W. Pugin's Drawings for the Church of St Vincent de Paul Liverpool, 1856–7

Dr Roderick O'Donnell, FSA, Inspector of Ancient Monuments and Historic Buildings for English Heritage, has kindly provided the following notes: A set of drawings signed 'E. W. Pugin architect' and dated 1856 and 7 which have recently come to light are now deposited in the Archdiocese of Liverpool archives. They are entitled 'St Vincent of [sic] Paul's church Liverpool in the diocese of Liverpool Revd B. O'Reilly'. The church is seen in the 'west elevation' (facing St James Street) and 'Side elevation' on Hardy Street, and in longitudinal and transverse cross-sections, which are untitled, but show the nave and chancel and the nave and aisles respectively. They evidently form a set for that priest to consider, giving him in two further drawings the plan of the church and the presbytery on one sheet and of the basement and second floor of the presbytery on another. The church is drawn very much as built, except for the north porch and attached octagonal baptistery, an unusual juxtaposition not proceeded with. Very characteristic of E. W. Pugin's emerging independent style is the height and attenuation of his proportions and the sharp angles of the many gables; the front onto St James Street has cross-gables fronting the aisles (which have lean-to roofs) and the east end chapels also have upstanding west-

facing gables with roundel windows. Big Geometric-
style tracery windows abound, especially the clerestory and massive west window, so that the church
was to be very well lit. The east end arrangements can
only be read on plan, and of the chancel only the arch
is shown on the section. The church and integral
presbytery are built right up on to the plot-line, and in
the church every square-inch is accounted for; the
benches are shown as mounted right up to the confessionals, the priests themselves having an external
corridor to the single and double confessional rooms
with fireplaces. This 'confessional aisle' (really a lean-
to threaded in-between the buttresses) also has stairs
up to a meeting room over the boys' sacristy. The
separate priests' sacristy is beyond from which they
could exit to follow on a line behind the side-altars and
the reredos behind the high altar (which appears only
on the dimensioned drawing, below) thus reaching a
longitudinal corridor within the house. The reredos,
screen-like wall, appears only on a drawing in another
hand which gives a scale and dimension. Statues are
marked against the chancel arch piers, the position of
the pulpit is handed round from that on the 'Revd
O'Reilly' plan and a porch internal lobby is shown at
the west (since that to the north was omitted). It shows
the church as built and as intended to be used: thus
this space under the organ gallery is also labelled as
'space for the poor' showing that even in this very poor
dockside congregation that Fr O'Reilly catered for
there were still to be some worse-off than others.

    In 1856–7 the 23 year old E. W. Pugin was also at
work building the nave at Belmont, and the cathedral
at Shrewsbury, to which this church most closely
relates. The style of the drawings is precise and

painstaking. However a pen and ink three-quarter view, probably intended for engraving for fund-raising, is done with much greater freedom. It is probably the earliest in the series, generalising for example on the bell-cote which in the 'Revd O'Reilly' drawings is much better worked out (and happily still surviving). Early E. W. Pugin drawings are rare, and this set shows him just about to burst the chrysalis of boyhood tutelage to his father's style and to blossom out as his own man, notably in the style and innovative planning of his church at Our Lady of Salette, Liverpool (1858–9).

BIBLIOGRAPHY

Burke, Thomas, *Catholic History of Liverpool*, Liverpool, C. Tinling, 1910.

Doyle, Peter, *Mitres and Missions in Lancashire*, Liverpool, The Bluecoat Press, 2005.

Hughes, J. Q., *Liverpool: City Building Series*, London, Studio Vista Ltd., 1969, p. 57.

Kennan, L.W., and McDonnell, J.T, *The Parish of St Vincent de Paul Centenary Booklet*, Liverpool, 1952.

Little, Bryan, *Catholic Churches since 1623*, London, Robert Hale, 1966.

Liverpool Heritage Bureau, *Buildings of Liverpool*, 1978, p. 67.

Martin, Christopher, *A Glimpse of Heaven*, Swindon, English Heritage, 2006.

O'Donnell, Roderick, 'Pugin, Edward Welby (1834–1875)', *Oxford Dictionary of National Biography*, Oxford University Press, 2004.

Pollard, R. and Pevsner, N., *The Buildings of England: Lancashire and the south west*, New Haven, Yale University Press, 2006.

The Builder, 19 April, 1856, p. 217
The Builder, 1 August, 1857, p. 452
The Tablet, 12 April 1856, p. 229
The Tablet, 28 February 1857, p. 131
The Tablet, 18 July 1857, p. 453
The Tablet, 19 August 1857, p. 548
The Tablet, 5 September 1857, p. 565
The Tablet, 8 May 1875, p. 596
Liverpool Roman Catholic Archdiocesan Archives.

ILLUSTRATIONS

DEAR SIR,

I REQUEST your attendance at a PUBLIC MEETING of the Catholics of Liverpool, to be held at the CLAYTON-HALL, Clayton Square, on TUESDAY, the 16th of May, at Seven o'Clock in the Evening, to take active measures for the ERECTION of the NEW CHURCH of ST. VINCENT OF PAUL.

I am, Dear Sir,

Yours sincerely in Christ,

✝ G. BROWN.

Liverpool, 5th May, 1854.

Figure 1: Bishop Brown's meeting to propose the building of St Vincent's.

At a PUBLIC MEETING of the CATHOLICS of LIVERPOOL, convened by the authority of the Right Reverend DR. BROWN, Bishop of Liverpool, and held at the CLAYTON HALL, on TUESDAY, 16th MAY, 1854, to take measures for the Erection of the NEW CHURCH OF ST. VINCENT OF PAUL, in one of the Poorest Districts in Liverpool.

THE RIGHT REVEREND DR. BROWN IN THE CHAIR;

It was Moved by J. B. ASPINALL, Esq., Seconded by The Very Reverend PROVOST CROOK, and *Resolved*—

That the Erection of a Catholic Church in the District of which New Bird Street is the centre, is a work of the highest order of Catholic Charity, the great number of Catholic Inhabitants, and the general poverty of the District, giving it especial claims upon the benevolence and consideration of the whole community.

Moved by RICHARD SHEIL, Esq., Seconded by the Rev. C. H. COLLINS, S.J., and *Resolved*,—

That recognising, as we do, that the Poor are at all times the particular objects to be cared for in God s Church, we determine to Build a Church in this District, and we urge on the whole community the importance of co-operating with their Venerated Bishop in a work so truly Catholic.

Moved by DANIEL POWELL, Esq., Seconded by the Rev. JAMES SHERIDAN, O.S.B., and *Resolved*,—

That, to carry out the foregoing Resolutions, a Subscription be now entered into, and that the following Gentlemen be requested to act as a Committee, to assist the Rev. BERNARD O'REILLY in Collecting Funds and Building the Church:—

CHAIRMAN—THE REV. B. O'REILLY.

MR. H. SHARPLES,	MR. JOHN YATES, JUN.,
MR. D. POWELL,	MR. G. LYNCH,
MR. J. B. ASPINALL,	MR. T. RYAN.

TREASURER—THE VERY REVEREND PROVOST CROOK.
SECRETARY—MR. THOMAS DALY.

[P. T. O.

Figure 2: Minutes of the public meeting where the decision is taken to build the new church.

New Church of St. Vincent of Paul,

LIVERPOOL.

I venture at this time, as an appropriate occasion, to put forth the claims which the great undertaking committed to my charge has upon the sympathy and support of the Catholic Body.

The District comprises the poor and densely-populated streets running between St. James's Street and the Docks. My flock numbers 7600 souls—two streets alone, New Bird Street and Brick Street, contain each 1200 Catholics.

For several years past we have made use of a miserable shed for the double purpose of Church and School, and have had to offer up the Holy Sacrifice in a building insufficient to keep out the wind and rain.

It so happens that whilst my flock consists of the poorest of the poor, land in the district is most costly, and it has been the work of years to obtain a site. I have, at last, with the blessing of God, been successful in securing one admirably adapted for the purpose, in the very centre of the district, and upon which I hope very shortly will stand the Church of "St. Vincent of Paul," another monument of Catholic progress and another evidence of the Catholic principle of caring for the poor.

I have not yet collected sufficient Funds for the Purchase of the Land, but as soon as this has been accomplished, I propose to commence Building the Church at once, relying upon the charitable support of the Public.

The undertaking has the warm sanction and approval of our venerated Bishops, who take an active interest in this effort to plant another Church amongst the poor, and who have been kindly pleased to point to it as a fitting object for the Charity of the Faithful during the Jubilee.

THE FOLLOWING IS AN EXTRACT FROM DR. BROWN'S JUBILEE PASTORAL.

" *You are fully aware of the very great want of a Church in that part of Liverpool near the Docks, known as the Church of St. Vincent of Paul. Notwithstanding all the efforts that have been made to procure the Funds necessary for erecting the intended Church, the amount required is far from being procured. On this account we recommend to all the Faithful to appropriate all their alms during the Jubilee, to the erection of the Church above-mentioned, as being the most meritorious good work to which at present they can be given.*"

Subscriptions will be gratefully received by the Very Rev. Dr. Crook, Warren Street, and by any of the other Clergy.

BERNARD O'REILLY.

32, *GREAT GEORGE STREET,*
29th October, 1854.

Figure 3: Fr O'Reilly's appeal for funds to construct the new church.

The Committee, in again calling the attention of Catholics to the importance of ministering to the urgent spiritual wants of a poor and densely-populated district like that in which it is proposed to erect the New Church, feel that they can scarcely add any thing to the admirable remarks of the Venerated Bishop of Liverpool, in his last Lental Pastoral on this subject. They will, however, again venture to remind the Catholic public, who have always cordially responded to appeals similar to the present, that a great number of poor Catholics have no means, or, at least, no other than those which will shortly be taken from them, of receiving the consolations of Religion, and hence of the great necessity there is for erecting a Church in the district referred to in the foregoing Resolutions.

The accommodation already provided is totally inadequate to receive the numbers of Catholics who should attend Divine Service, and there is no doubt that unfortunately too many of the poorer classes of Catholics attempt to justify their lukewarmness and neglect of their religious duties, on the plea that there is no room for them in the Churches already erected. To those not acquainted with the circumstances, it may be proper to state, that the district in question is one in which the Epidemic of 1847 raged with the greatest virulence, and where many of those estimable Clergy, who, like their great Master laid down their lives for their flocks, caught the disease which hurried them to the grave. The temporary building in which the large number of poor Catholics who inhabit the district in question meet to assist at the Holy Sacrifice, is about to be taken away from them in consequence of the termination of the lease, and thus they will be deprived of the means of performing their religious duties, unless some steps be at once taken in their regard. The Building itself is of the very poorest description, not protecting the congregation even from the inclemency of the elements. The Committee, therefore, confidently appeal to that generosity and Catholic spirit which, in this diocese, and more particularly in Liverpool, have raised so many Churches and Schools to the honour and glory of Almighty God. They feel that they have only plainly and truthfully to lay before those Catholics, whom God has blessed with wealth and prosperity, the spiritual necessities of their poor brethren in the faith, to induce them readily to come to their assistance, and to perform a duty the most pleasing to Almighty God, and the most honourable to his creatures, viz.:— that of raising a Temple to his glory. Though above £1800 have been already collected or promised, yet the value of the land in the neighbourhood where it is proposed to build the Church is so high, that this amount will not suffice to pay for the land alone.

Contributions will be gratefully received by the Rev. BERNARD O'REILLY, 32, Great George Street; the Very Rev. Provost CROOK, 16, Warren Street, Liverpool; or by any Member of the Committee.

B. O'REILLY, CHAIRMAN.

Figure 4: Fr O'Reilly's committee appeals for funds to erect the new church.

34, GREAT GEORGE STREET,

LIVERPOOL, *April* 2, 1856.

We have great pleasure in informing you that the FIRST STONE of the NEW CHURCH of ST. VINCENT OF PAUL, St. James' Street, will be solemnly BLESSED and LAID by the BISHOP OF LIVERPOOL, on TUESDAY NEXT, April 8th, the Transferred Feast of St. Patrick.

The Ceremony will commence at Eleven o'clock.

May we request the honour of your company, and beg your support upon the occasion.

We are,

Yours very faithfully in Christ,

BERNARD O'REILLY,

RICHARD SEED,

PETER HOLMES.

P.S.—A LUNCH will be provided immediately after the Ceremony, at the Royal Assembly Rooms, Great George Street. Tickets, 3s. 6d. each.

Figure 5: Invitation to the laying of the foundation stone.

LIST of SUBSCRIPTIONS RECEIVED at the MEETING, the great Majority of the Subscribers having already given largely.

Name	£	s.	d.	Name	£	s.	d.
Mr. M. Macklin	100	0	0	Mr. John Browne	5	0	0
" H. Sharples	50	0	0	" J. Quinn	5	0	0
" D. Powell	50	0	0	" Haggerty	3	0	0
" R. Sheil	30	0	0	" J. O. Wood	2	2	0
" J. Gibson	20	0	0	" James Reade	2	0	0
" R. Cusker	20	0	0	" B. Mahon	2	0	0
A Gentleman	10	0	0	" S. Burns	2	0	0
Mr. E. Dunne	10	0	0	Rev. E. J. Bradshaw	1	10	0
" R. Dunne	10	0	0	Mr. J. C. Griffin	1	1	0
" T. Darwin	10	0	0	" William Connolly	1	1	0
" J. Yates, Jun	10	0	0	" William Splaine	1	0	0
Messrs. Rockliff & Sons	10	0	0	Rev. Thomas Kelly	1	0	0
Mr. Peter Garvey	10	0	0	Mr. Owen M'Kenna	1	0	0
" Jameson	6	0	0	" James Reade, Jun	1	0	0
" J. Mullins	5	5	0	Very Rev. John Canon Walmsley	1	0	0
" W. Baynes	5	0	0	Mr. P. O'Keefe	1	0	0
" J. B. Aspinall	5	0	0	" Stephen Benyille	1	0	0
" F. Moynagh	5	0	0	" O'Donnell	1	0	0
S. H.	5	0	0	" P. Lynch	1	0	0
Mr. J. Lennon	5	0	0	" V. J. Verbraeken	1	0	0
Messrs. G. & J. Lynch	5	0	0	" M. Rice	1	0	0
Mr. T. Carroll	5	0	0	Rev. Jas. Sheridan	1	0	0
" B. Traynor	5	0	0	Mr. Jas. Clarke	1	0	0
" E. Kelly	5	0	0	" Rourke	1	0	0
" J. Doyle	5	0	0	" Giacomo Lertroi	1	0	0
" G. Stewart	5	0	0	" Charles Crangle	0	10	0
" T. Daly	5	0	0	" J. Newton	0	5	0
" D. Bannon	5	0	0				
" M. Carney	5	0	0		£476	14	0
" R. H. Sheil	5	0	0	Sundry Collections at Meeting	8	0	11½
" W. Bunbury	5	0	0				
" W. Reynolds	5	0	0		£484	14	11½

Previous to the Meeting the amount in hand was £2799 13 5
Sum promised before Meeting 352 0 0

£3151 13 5

To this amount, of course, will have to be added, the amount promised and received at the Meeting.

Figure 6: Some first subscriptions for the church.

St. Vincent of Paul's,

Hardy Street, Liverpool.

DEAR REV. SIR,

I have great pleasure in forwarding to you
the enclosed Notice of the Opening of the New Church
of St. Vincent of Paul.

May I beg the favour of your presence on the
occasion.

You will please to bring Surplice, Cassock and
Birretta.

I am directed by the BISHOP OF LIVERPOOL to
express his wish that all the Regular Clergy should appear
in the habit of their respective order.

A LUNCHEON will be provided at the Royal Assembly
Rooms, Great George Street, for which I shall be happy
to present you with a Ticket, and I shall deem it a favour
would you kindly intimate to me if it is your intention
to be present.

I am, Dear Rev. Sir,

Yours very faithfully in Christ,

BERNARD O'REILLY.

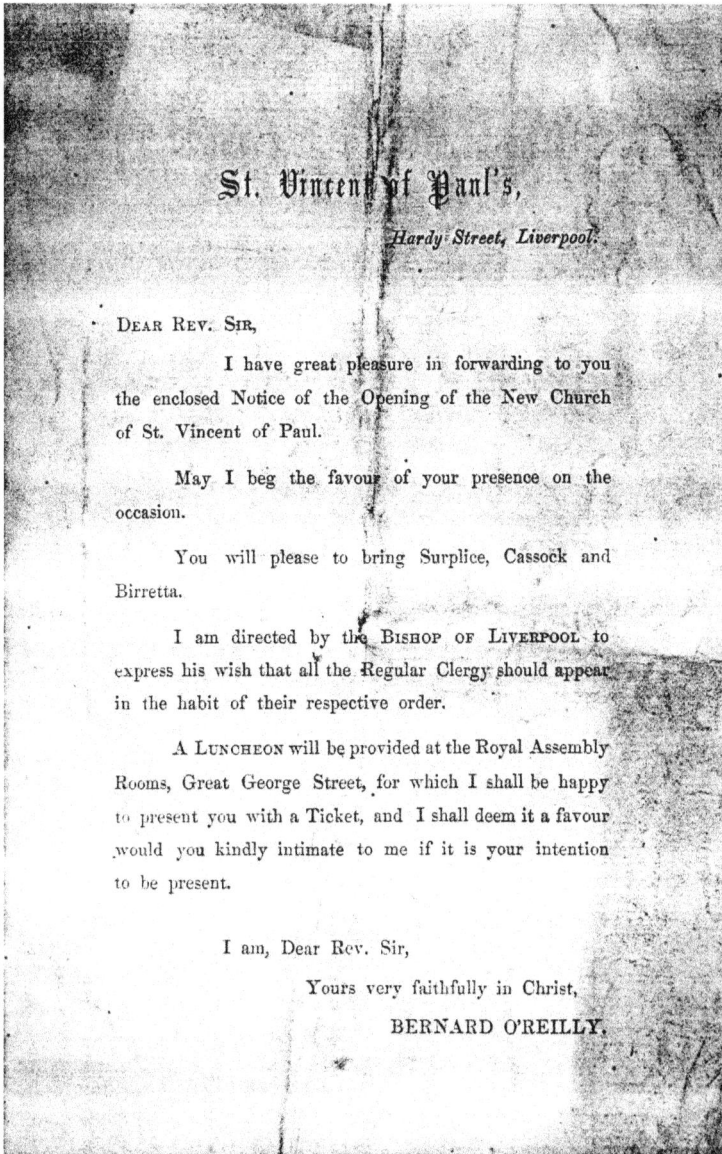

Figure 7: Invitation to the opening of the church.

SOLEMN OPENING
OF THE

New Church of St. Vincent of Paul,

ST. JAMES' STREET.

ON WEDNESDAY, AUG. 26, 1857,

THIS CHURCH WILL BE OPENED
BY THE

Lord Bishop of Liverpool,

WITH SOLEMN MASS.

IN PRESENCE OF THE FOLLOWING PRELATES AND DIGNITARIES:—

THE MOST REVEREND THE ARCHBISHOP OF DUBLIN,
THE RIGHT REVEREND THE COADJUTOR OF DROMORE,
THE RIGHT REVEREND THE BISHOP OF SALFORD,
THE RIGHT REVEREND THE BISHOP OF SHREWSBURY,
THE RIGHT REVEREND THE BISHOP OF NOTTINGHAM,
THE VERY REVEREND THE CHAPTER OF LIVERPOOL,
THE VERY REVEREND THE CHAPTER OF SALFORD,
THE VERY REVEREND THE CHAPTER OF SHREWSBURY.

HIGH MASS TO COMMENCE AT ELEVEN O'CLOCK.

THE SERMON WILL BE PREACHED BY

THE RIGHT REVEREND DR. LEAHY,

COADJUTOR BISHOP OF DROMORE.

PONTIFICAL VESPERS AND GRAND BENEDICTION
AT HALF-PAST SIX O'CLOCK.

Sermon by The Right Reverend The Bishop of Shrewsbury.

Haydn's Mass, No. 3, will be Sung with full Choir and Orchestral Accompaniments, under the direction of Mr. J. RICHARDSON, Organist of the Pro-Cathedral.

TICKETS OF ADMISSION:—

To the Morning Service, 10s., 5s., 2s. 6d. To the Evening Service, 2s. 6d. 1s., 6d. May be had at the Presbytery, Hardy Street; from Messrs. ROCKLIFF & SON, 44, Castle Street; and from all the Catholic Booksellers.

A LUNCHEON will be provided after Morning Service, at the Royal Assembly Rooms, Great George Street. Tickets, 3s. 6d., to be had from the above.

ROCKLIFF AND SON, PRINTERS, 44, CASTLE STREET, LIVERPOOL.

Figure 8: Solemn opening handbill.

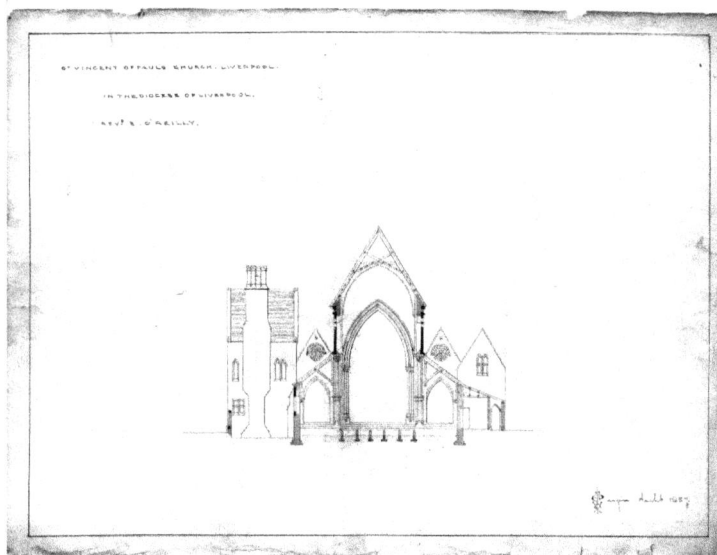

Figure 9: E. W. Pugin, Cross section looking west.

Figure 10: E. W. Pugin, Elevation of west front.

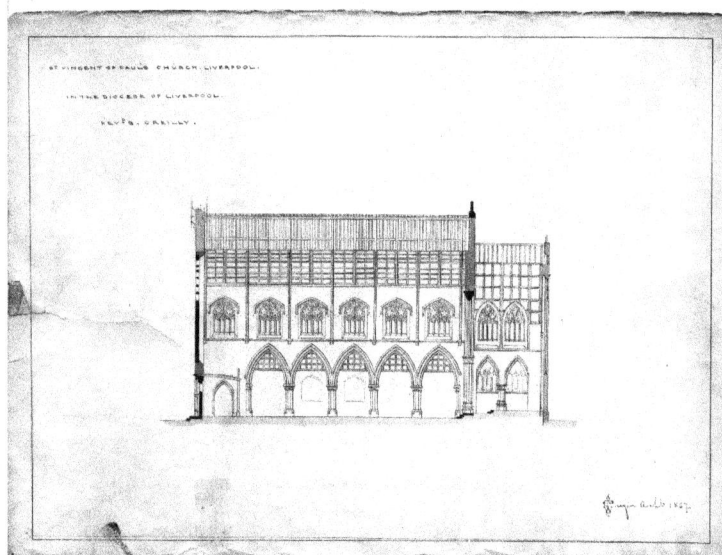

Figure 11: E. W. Pugin, Cross section of nave and chancel from south.

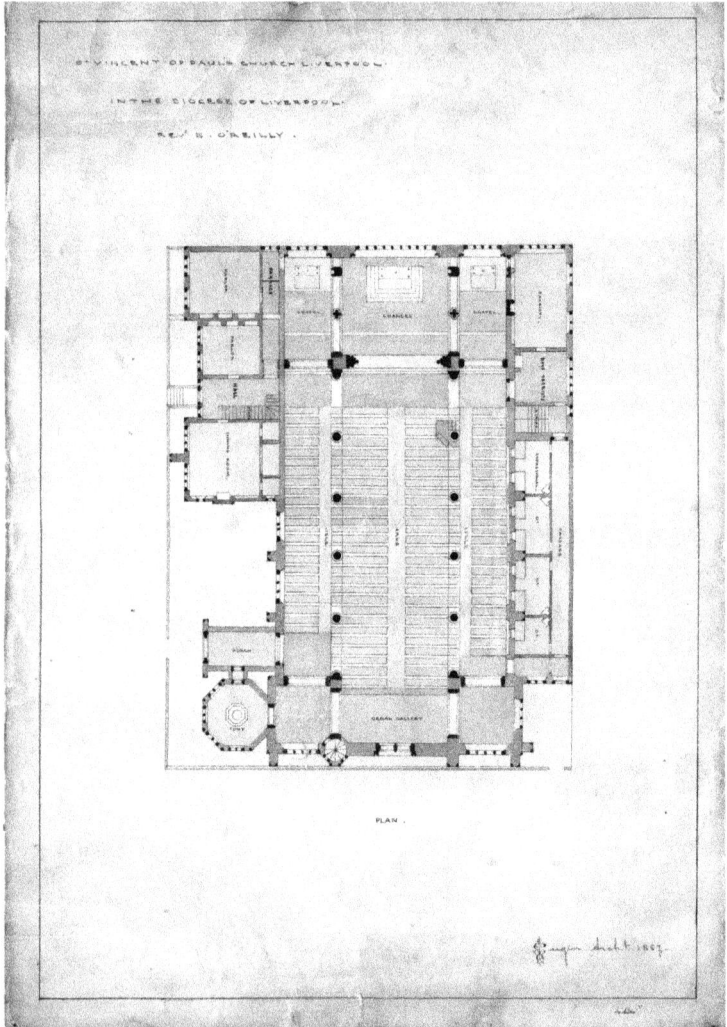

Figure 12: E. W. Pugin, Ground plan of church and presbytery.

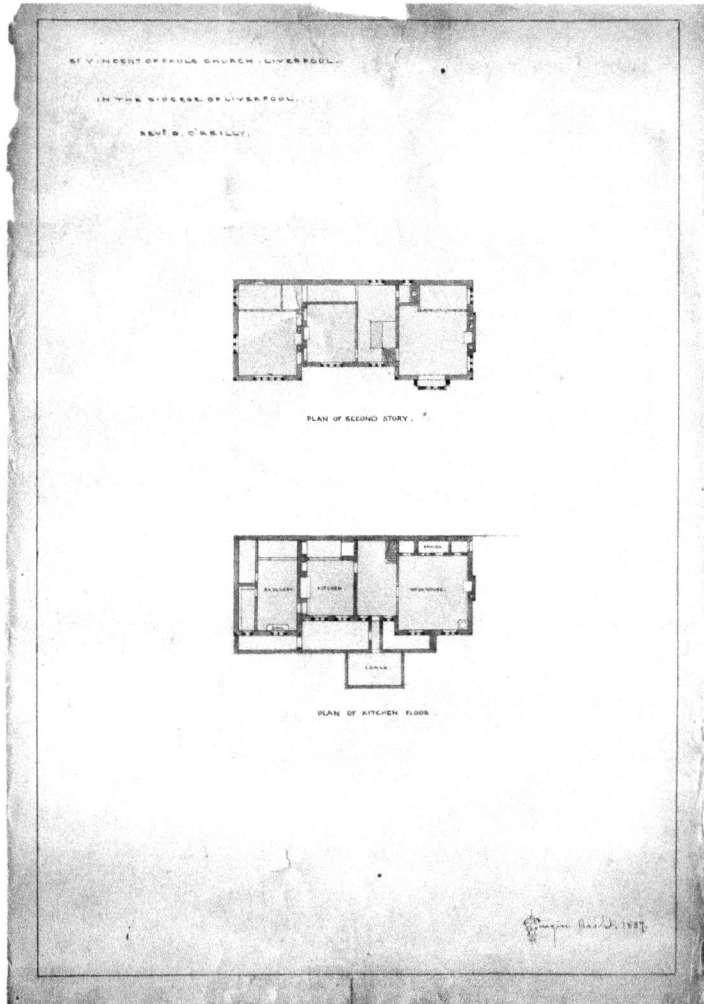

Figure 13: E. W. Pugin, *Plan of kitchen floor and second storey.*

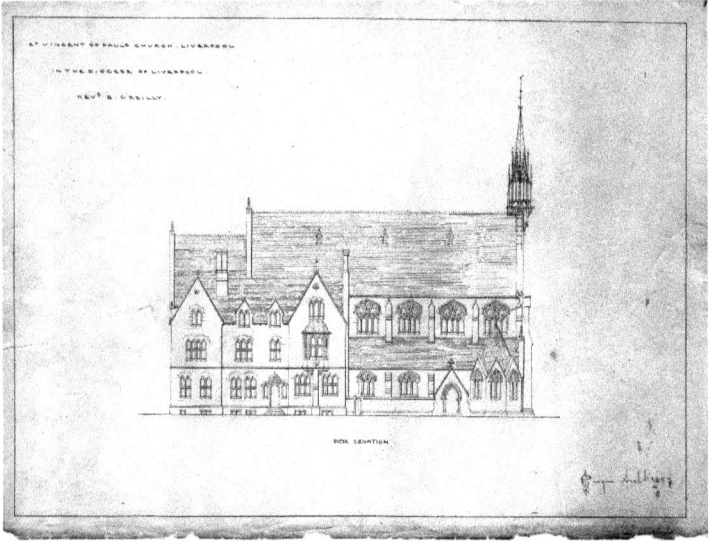

Figure 14: E. W. Pugin, North elevation of church and presbytery.

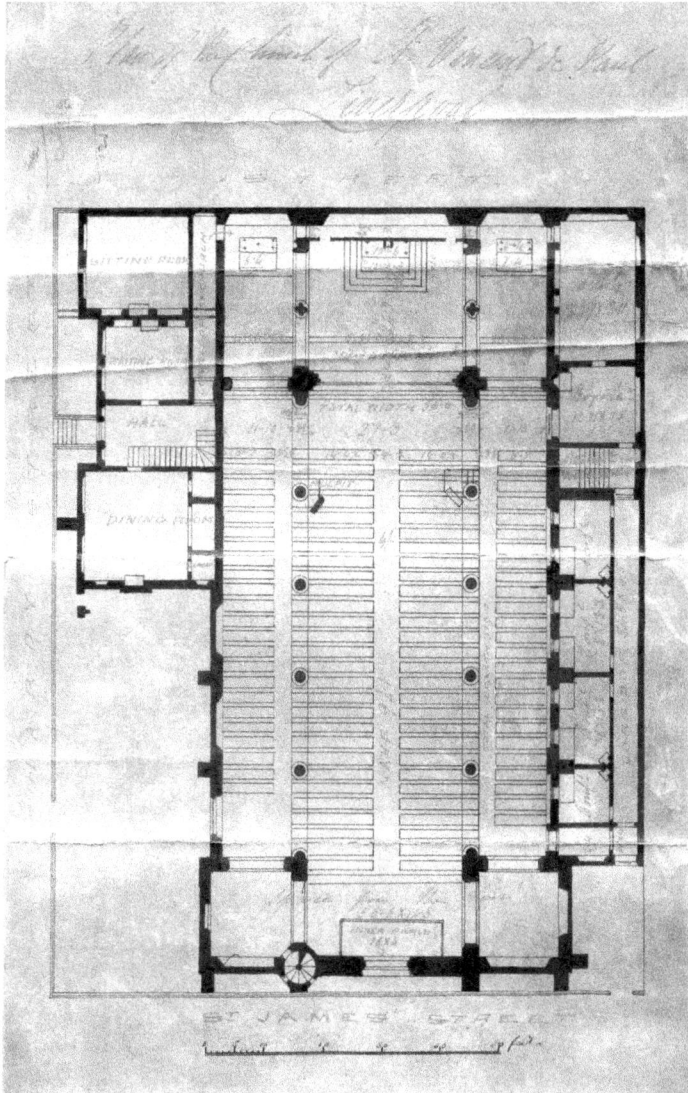

Figure 15: E. W. Pugin, *Ground plan of church and presbytery.*
The Baptistery does not appear on this plan. Contrast with Figure 12.

Figure 16: E. W. Pugin: Perspective view of the west front, north side and presbytery.

Figure 17: West front, north side and presbytery, 2012.

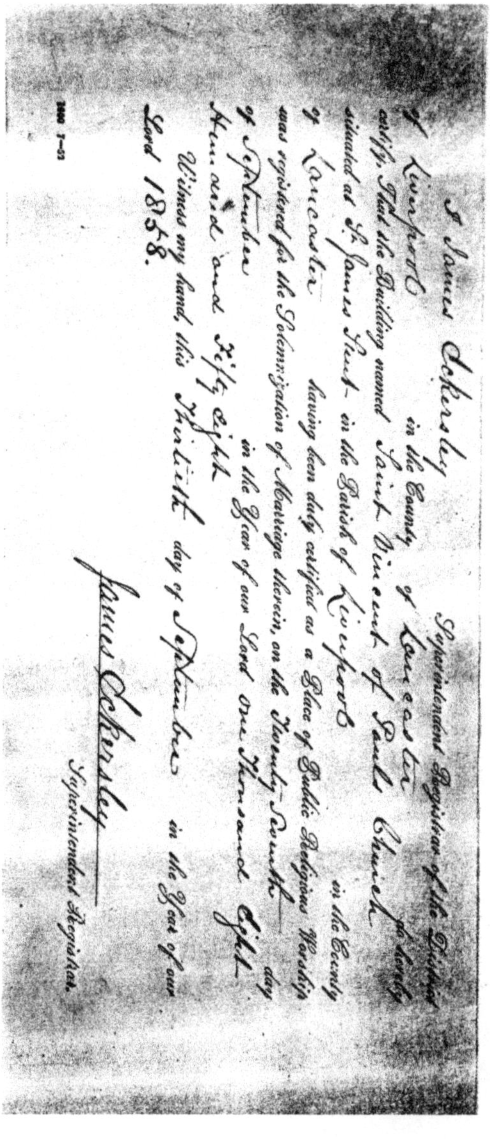

I James Eckersley Superintendent Registrar of the District of Liverpool in the County of Lancaster do hereby certify That the Building named Saint Vincent of Paul Church situated at St James Street in the Parish of Liverpool in the County of Lancaster having been duly certified as a Place of Public Religious Worship was registered for the Solemnization of Marriages therein, on the Twenty Seventh day of September in the Year of our Lord One Thousand Eight Hundred and Fifty eight

Witness my hand, this Thirtieth day of September in the Year of our Lord 1858.

James Eckersley
Superintendent Registrar.

Figure 18: James Eckersley, Superintendent Registrar, licenses St. Vincent's for the solemnization of weddings.

Figure 19: Coat of Arms of Bishop George Brown.

Figure 20: Sculpted Coat of Arms of
Bishop George Brown in Sanctuary, 2012.

Figure 21: Sculpted Coat of Arms of
Bishop Alexander Goss in Sanctuary, 2012.

Figure 22: Coat of Arms of Bishop Alexander Goss.

Figure 23: Coat of Arms of Bishop Bernard O'Reilly.

Figure 24: Chancel. The sculpted heads of Bishop Brown and Bishop Goss
can be seen on either side, beneath their respective Coats of Arms, 2012.

*Figure 25: East window and chancel,
viewed from the organ gallery, 2012.*

Figure 26: Interior, west window and organ gallery, 2012.

Figure 27: Lady Altar, 2012.

Figure 28: St Joseph's Altar, 2012.

Figure 29: A view of the south aisle from a 1920's postcard.

Figure 30: The south aisle, 2012.

Figure 31: The presbytery, 2012.

Figure 32: The pulpit, 2012.

Figure 33: The baptismal font, 2012.

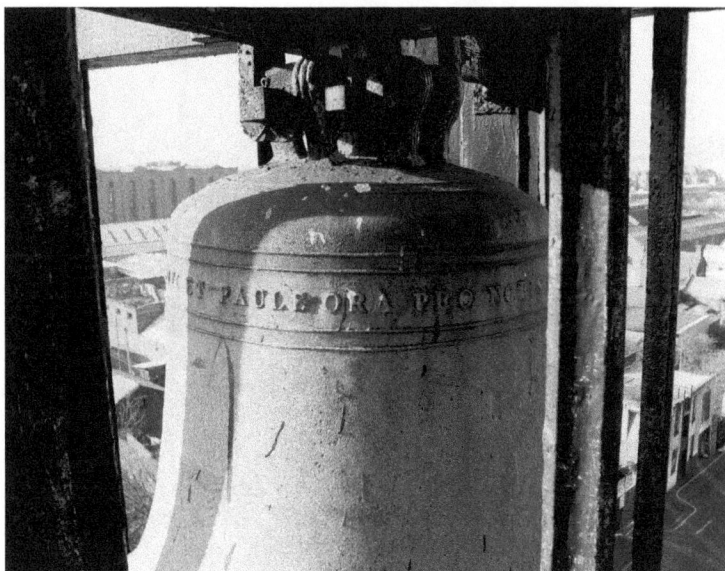

Figure 34: The inscription on the bell reads, 'Sancte Vincenti et Paule Ora Pro Nobis', 2012.

Figure 35: The cross at the top of the belfry spire, 2012.

Figure 36: Carved stonework at the base of the belfry, 2012.

Figure 37: One of the four metal dragons
guarding the base of the belfry, 2012.

Figure 38: Archbishop Patrick Kelly studying Bishop O'Reilly's sculpted head at the West door, 2012.